and TALES

Fishing Tips and Tales

A collection of Short Stories

C. William King

This is a work of fiction. Names, characters, businesses, places, events and incidents either are the products of the author's imagination or used in a fictitious manner. Any resemblance to actual persons, living or dead, or actual events is purely coincidental.

FISHING TIPS AND TALES

Copyright © 2017 by C. William King

All Illustrations Copyright © 2015 by Roberta J. Jarc - www.JarcArt.com

ISBN-13: 978-1544194578
ISBN-10: 1544194579

First Edition: February 27, 2017

Table of Contents

Acknowledgements

I would like to thank all my fishing friends for putting up with my tall tales, bad habits, and other indiscretions while on fishing trips. I learned a lot from all of you, some more than others.

I am indebted to my uncle, Paul Kane, who taught me my first fishing skills with worms and bobbers, when I was six years old; John Barnhart who urged me to start attending fishing club meetings; Ron Mankowski who taught me how to tie my first fly, a black wooly bugger, Jeff Wagner, who encouraged me to read the bamboo rod building books of Wayne Cattanach, Everett Garrison and Hoagy Carmichael, and George Maurer and Bernard Elser: and Russ Gooding who suggested I study the 'Bamboo Rod Restoration Handbook' by Michael Sinclair.

I am grateful to Roberta Jarc for sharing her wonderful fly plates that illustrate this book.

My thanks to Anne Bauswein for editing, short story teacher June Bolenbaugh, for helping with early drafts of many stories, and to Jack FitzGerald and all those who read the final drafts of the entire manuscript and made helpful suggestions.

Finally, I am overwhelmed with the love and joy in my life from my wife, children, their spouses, and all my grandchildren.

Preface

This book is a fictionalized memoir. Most of the stories are based upon a real incident, although the dialog has been invented to move the story along. The names of people, places and things have been changed to preclude any lawsuits. These stories are told with a wink and a nod to the best traditions of fishing tales found in literature, and told in local watering holes, on fishing trips, around campfires, in wilderness lodges, and in fishing clubs and organizations everywhere.

Tinkersville Tips and Tales

I am a fly fisherman who enjoys tying his own flies. I make a large variety of realistic looking aquatic and flying insects in my basement with a tying vice, a large magnifying glass, and a few tools such as tiny pliers and scissors, using only small hooks, thread, and bits of fur and feathers. One spring day, I trekked out to the hunting and fishing store in my hometown for materials to make some new fly patterns. The fly fishing section is relatively small, and often seems to be out of, or not carry, the exact items that I want. I often end up buying something that I did not come in for, and then ordering the stuff I do want from a catalog. But this visit garnered a jackpot. It was a midweek evening and the person behind the cash register this time was about 18 years old. When he saw I was buying fly tying items his face lit up.

"Are you a fly fisherman?" he asked.
"Yes," I replied.

He said that his name was Mike and his family owns a cabin on Oak Creek near Tinkersville. He was a fly fisherman, too, and when he was there a few days ago, the trout were biting like crazy. He gave me directions and told me what patterns the trout were hitting on while he was ringing up my purchases.

"You oughta go," he urged, as I collected my change.
"Thanks a lot." I walked out of the store, unsure of whether I was thanking him for the transaction or the tip.

While walking into the parking lot, I mulled over what just happened. This information was too good to ignore, and there was just something about his natural enthusiasm and earnestness that made me decide on the spot to give it a try. As I climbed into the car, it hit me. I could not believe I was taking fishing advice from someone who is one-third my age and looked like he did not need to shave every day. Perhaps though, it was a good thing that he was young. Most older (and wiser) fly fisherman would *never* give away a hot fishing spot. Why would he give a complete stranger fishing tips anyway? Maybe it was a fellowship of fly fisherman kind of thing, or maybe I just looked like his grandfather.

When I got home from the store, I immediately called up my fishing buddy, Rodger, and asked him if he wanted to go to a really hot spot. "I don't know. The boss has some things for me to do this weekend," Rodger said. But he did not sound exactly enthusiastic about the things he needed to do. I said that I had family commitments Saturday evening, too.

"Why don't we just go early Saturday morning and plan to be back by about 5:00 PM? That way we can go fishing and still fit other things into our weekend schedules. It doesn't have to take all weekend." Then I told him how I got my tip.

"Well, in that case, I would be more than happy to go with you," Rodger said. Actually, I know Rodger pretty well. Never once did I have to twist his arm to go fishing. He would have gone anyway, no matter how I got my tip. We had been on many previous trips together and trusted each other's instincts.

To pass the time while driving long distances on previous fishing trips, we would tell each other fishing tales, some of which were even approximately true. By now, he knew all of mine and I knew all his. This was a new tale, so it was probably true. At least he was sure that I was convinced. Furthermore, this stream was close to Petroleum Creek and Petroleum Creek flowed through a state park of the same name near there. It was known to have some good fishing spots, so we would probably do well. We set the date for the coming weekend, so as not to miss whatever action was happening.

As it turned out, Oak Creek was out-of-state, and neither Rodger nor I had a fishing license. The time was too short to get one by mail. Our fishing store did not sell out-of-state fishing licenses, and internet purchase of fishing licenses was still in the future. We would have to get one on the way to the stream. I called ahead and verified that a sporting goods store in Tinkersville could sell us the state fishing license and trout stamp.

Luckily, I had all the fly tying materials I needed on hand and spent the next several nights happily tying up the flies we would need for the trip. I hoped that the tip I had gotten this time would yield many big fish. I had visions of eager trout furiously striking at my flies. Maybe that is the reason some of them are not as perfect as I would hope! I had the tip about which flies were working at that locale, so I tried especially hard to tie good ones. I tied some of them sparse, and some full, and made a variety of sizes, shapes and subtle color variations. Trout can be very selective, but with a tip this specific, one or more of them would certainly work. The night before our departure, I carefully downloaded driving maps into my GPS and programmed the route, sure that we could drive right up to the magic spot.

The day arrived and I picked Rodger up early in the morning. The sporting goods store opened at 8:30AM, so we timed the two and one-half trip to Tinkersville to allow time to eat breakfast, buy our licenses, and then go to the stream. My GPS said that the fishing spot was only two miles outside of town. We arrived in Tinkersville and ate breakfast at the Arcadian, the town's small breakfast and lunch cafe. When we drove up to the cafe, we noticed many cars parked in the street out in front of the place - a good sign. I love to visit these places. The food is always good, the service friendly, the prices reasonable, and most importantly, the bathroom is warm and clean. (I have learned over time to appreciate the importance of these small comforts when on a fishing trip.) I noticed that the sporting goods store where we would purchase our fishing licenses was next door. It was closed, but we took the opportunity to peer through the front window. The merchandise in the window display, mostly high school athletic equipment, looked faded and bleached from the sun - like it had been there undisturbed for many summers. No matter. We would be going in for licenses.

Rodger and I entered the café. The counter stools and most of the tables in the place were already filled, so we sat down at one of the few empty tables near the door. As we looked around, we noticed that the place was brightly decorated in Coca Cola memorabilia. We were dressed like everyone else in the place - in flannel shirts, denim jeans, and boots - but as soon as the patrons saw us, we could tell that they knew we were outsiders. They were telling jokes and stories and calling to each other from table to table. They were all regulars, and everyone in the place knew every other person, except us. Whenever we caught someone looking at us, we just smiled back in a friendly way and tried to act like we were good ole' boys ourselves, just from somewhere else.

"Whata yah Gents have today?" asked the waitress with a pencil poised over a small order pad. She was smiling at us expectantly, and wore a white apron over a gingham-checked dress.

"I'll have the pancakes," I responded, believing an old Boy Scout axiom that carbohydrates for breakfast make good fuel for strenuous outdoor days. Rodger ordered the 'belly buster', which included two of about everything on the breakfast menu. After devouring the hearty fare, draining our coffee cups and paying the waitress, we left to get our fishing licenses.

We walked next door to the sporting goods store. The store looked like it opened in the 1920s or '30s and had not been remodeled or cleaned since. The floor was wooden and creaked when we walked across it. I think it creaked every time we shifted weight from foot to foot, too. The ceiling was in shadow, high over our heads. It was covered with two-by-two foot dark gray tin metal squares with a repeating intricate pattern. It was apparent from a ceiling repair near the wall where the grime had been disturbed, that the squares were white when new. The glass display cases were filled with really old fishing supplies and covered in dust. Stacked on top were piles of seemingly newer merchandise, which obscured most of the contents of the cases.

Our eyes adjusted to the relative dimness of the store, and we noticed the owner-proprietor in the back, standing behind an old wooden counter with a mechanical cash register on one side of it and a green felt pad on the other. He was tall, thin and had a shock of white hair. He looked even older than the store.

"We need out-of-state fishing licenses," I said, handing him our identification. Silently he took our drivers' licenses and spent a very long time hand copying the information.

"Sign here," he rumbled, pointing to a line at the bottom of the form, then added, "That'll be sixty dollars each." Each of us handed him a credit card.

He took one look at us and said, "Don't take credit cards. Never did, never will."

I dug in my wallet and found the sixty dollars. Rodger looked in his wallet and then at me.

"I don't have that much," he said. I loaned Rodger the balance, counting the remaining money in my wallet, figuring at that point of the trip that I was going to buy both of us lunch, too. Rodger and I had always split expenses evenly on our fishing trips, but this one looked like it was going to be an exception. Well, I thought, what are friends for anyway? After the transaction, the proprietor studied us for a moment.

"Where you boys going?" he asked. We explained that we were fly fisherman, had never fished near here before, and were following a tip. We told him we were going to Oak Creek.

He turned his head slightly and squinted at us out of the corners of his eyes as if to size us up. After a slight pause, he said "You boys don't really want to go there. Hard place to find. No parking. The stream is narrow and covered with lots o' tree branches hangin' out over the holes. Difficult place to fly fish. Lots o' better places nearby. Why don't you go to the state park about two miles south of here?" He gave us directions and added "The creek flows through wide fields, easy to cast, lots o' people, parking lots, picnics. You'd be a lot better off." We thanked him for his tip and directions, then walked out of the store and over to the car.

"You know he looks like he's fished around these parts for decades, and probably knows every fisherman and every fishing spot for miles around, but what he said just doesn't sound right to me," I said to Rodger.

"Yeah, if I was a fish, I would want to hide under a log or leafy branch in the shade. Not swim in full view of predators or the general public," Rodger said.

We decided to follow the original tip. The GPS quickly took us out of town and to a bridge over Petroleum Creek. After a few turns, we turned left onto a gravel road with no name on it. We saw no stream, no signs, and we could only drive about five miles an hour due to the potholes and ruts.

I turned to Rodger. "I hope this isn't a wild goose chase. Maybe the old guy was right." We rounded a bend in the road and saw six vehicles parked along the road or partially on it. There were two old campers, two beat-up pickup trucks and two badly rusted cars. They all had in-state license plates and looked like locals. We drove up behind them, pulling the car off the road as much as possible. A path worn in the weeds led downhill. This had to be it. We got out of the car, put on our waders and vests, and strung up our rods.

"Here are some of the flies that I tied," I said to Rodger holding out my hand with an assortment of fly patterns on it.
"These ought to work just fine," I added, hoping that this was true. We carefully added the flies to our fly boxes, packed them in our vests and moved off.

The woods in late spring were magnificent. New shoots were pushing up through damp, dead leaves all over the forest floor, and the leaves on the trees were just unfurling, but had not fully leafed out yet. The new green color of spring was everywhere. The overhead canopy was not quite full and we could catch glimpses of the sun low in the bright morning sky, which was covered with high cirrus clouds. The air was cool and carried with it a hint of wild fragrances. There was little or no wind, which is perfect for fly fishing. We found the stream only 150 yards away. It was a typical picturesque mountain trout stream with just the right amount of riffles and crystal clear pools. Occasionally we could see trout swimming around. We made our way through the woods upstream and saw only two other fishermen the whole day. The fishermen from the other cars had evidently gone downstream.

The creek meandered and, since we had never been there before, Rodger and I decided to walk along the stream for a few hundred yards to check where the stream rushed over shallow areas, and where it leisurely pooled. We moved quietly and cautiously, staying well away from the edge of the water to avoid spooking the trout. Most of the pools were framed by branches hanging out over their edges with leaves draping to within inches of the water level.

Rodger pointed with the tip of his rod at the deep end of a pool in the dark shade of overhanging trees and whispered, "Looks like a likely place for a trout to hide. How is your roll casting?"

"I guess we'll find out," I whispered back, wondering how I would cast a fly in there.

A roll cast is used when there is an obstruction directly behind the fisherman and there is no room for the backcast. In the roll cast, the fisherman must keep all parts of the line in front of him at all times. This necessitates a shortened back stroke and forward power stroke making it more difficult to cast a fly accurately. Not willing to struggle with roll casting this early in the day, I murmured to Rodger,
"Maybe there is an easier place to fish farther upstream. Let's keep walking."

As we continued walking along the stream, Rodger spotted a tiny rivulet trickling down the steep hillside on the opposite bank of the stream. It made a wonderful light tinkling and splashing sound as it made its way down the rocks to the creek.

"Look at that pool under the waterfall. This looks like a great spot to start," Rodger said. Since Rodger had found his starting point, I decided to fish the next likely area upstream, a tongue of sand and gravel on the inside of a horseshoe-shaped bend. On the opposite side of the stream, the water had undercut the bank and a fairly large tree had fallen into the water. Parts of the trunk and larger branches were under the water level, but many branches were above. From the trunk's state of decay, it looked like this had happened a few years ago. The underwater branches created a boundary between the swifter flowing current in the center of the stream and a pocket of relatively slow moving water behind them. This phenomenon is well known to fishermen as a seam.

"What a perfect place for trout to hide!" I thought to myself. *"The motion of the current around the bend would deliver food to a hungry trout lying in wait, or the trout could rest in the relatively slow-moving water behind the trunk and branches."*

The small peninsula of sand and gravel was covered in tufts of small grass-like plants, and behind me, the border of large trees was a good distance from the edge of the stream. I would not have to worry about my backcast getting snagged, but placing my fly in and among the tree branches without being hung up would be a big challenge.

Because there were few insects over the stream at this time of day, I decided to start fishing with a nymph pattern, the aquatic stage in the life cycle of some insects. I was careful to select something from among the flies I tied for this place. For my first few casts, I let my nymph dead-drift past the submerged tree limbs about a foot below the water surface. I pulled my wrap-around polarized sunglasses from my fishing vest and put them on. The polarization and the clarity of the water allowed me to see trout rising from the invisible depths to the level of my nymph pattern. They tracked it for a few feet before turning away. I was quietly excited and filled with anticipation. With just these few casts, I knew this was a good place. On the very next cast, I gave the nymph a life-like motion, tugging it gently as it traveled downstream. This did the trick, and a nice brown trout swam rapidly into view and attacked the nymph.

I set the hook and turned his head with pressure from my rod to one side, so when he ran, it would not be back into the underwater tree branches where I knew I would lose him. He headed off downstream where I could play him for a few minutes and then reel him in. I used a one-and-a-half-pound tippet, so there was no real danger of him breaking the line as long as I did nothing stupid. He was thirteen inches long and a real beauty. I held him over my head for a moment to show Rodger, who was barely visible through the trees. Rodger waved his arm in acknowledgment. I am one of those people who believe that Lee Wulff, a famous fisherman and conservationist, was right when he declared, "Trout are too valuable to be only caught once." So I quickly released the trout, and after a moment, he swam briskly away and disappeared downstream. He would survive being caught, and I wished him well.

We had a great few hours fishing, moving up and down the stream, and I did have to use my roll casting. Some trout were hiding exactly where Rodger had pointed them out earlier in the day. The fish were hungry, the fly patterns I tied worked, and the steam conditions could not have been better. At one point, a school of browns were fighting each other for the right to eat my nymph pattern. Then I caught one that was an unusually strong fighter, whose struggles spooked the other fish. In all, I caught five trout; Rodger caught three. Most of them had wintered over for more than one year. It was both exciting and deeply satisfying at the same time. For good measure, I pushed the position capture button on my GPS so we could come back to this exact position on the stream in the future.

As we fished, the sun climbed higher in the sky. I looked up and noticed that the clouds had departed and sky had become brighter. In bright sunshine conditions, trout lose interest in feeding, so we decided to call it quits at about 2:00 PM. This was a critical time because we had to start for home soon, and the café had a sign that said they closed at 2:30 PM. We wanted to get back for food and creature comforts before they closed.

We made it back just in time before closing and ordered. While waiting for our food, our thoughts went back to the store proprietor. Why did he want to send us somewhere else? Normally, if you buy your fishing license in a local store, courtesy and custom requires some level of truthfulness on the part of the proprietor. It was a small town. If six local people were fishing there, he had to know. But everything else in his story matched. Then it dawned on us; he was saving the best place for the local fisherman.

After we finished eating, it was past the café's closing time. We thanked the cook and the waitress for staying open for us, and gave them especially large tips. By this time, we decided to thank the old proprietor, too.

We left the café and walked into the sporting goods store. He was still there.
"Remember us?" I asked. "You sold us our fishing licenses this morning and gave us a fishing tip on where to go."
"Yep," he said warily, slowly nodding his head.
"Your tip was fantastic. We caught eight trout between us," I declared with a big grin.
"Your fishing tip *was* fantastic," said Rodger, nodding in enthusiastic agreement.
"All we can say is thank you, thank you," I added. He looked stunned, but recovered quickly.
"Exactly where did you boys go?" he asked.

I did not know what to say; we had not followed his directions. Rodger jumped right in.

"Only two miles from here, exactly where you told us to go! Come on, let's get on the road. And thanks again." Before the proprietor could ask for any more details, Rodger turned around and pushed me out the door in front of him.

We left the store in a rush, and when we walked down the sidewalk a few steps and out of eyesight of the proprietor, we laughed out loud. We could not stop grinning and talking about our adventure the whole two and one-half hour drive back.

"This was a pretty good day!" I said pulling into Rodger's driveway to drop him off.

"A very good day indeed," he agreed as he stepped out of the car. I helped Rodger unload his fishing gear. "Yes," I thought to myself, "It was a really great day for fishing tips and tales."

The Best Fishing Club Meeting I Ever Attended

I belong to the Central Lakes Fishing Association (CLFA). It is an area fishing club, which averages about three hundred dues-paying members. The remarkably large number probably indicates that fishing must be pretty good in the Central Lakes area. The club is made up of both men and women, from teenagers to octogenarians. The purpose of the club is to promote conservation and the sport of fishing, but I think most members are there to get an edge on catching the biggest and largest number of game fish that they can. Fifty to seventy-five people show up for most CLFA meetings.

I remember taking my fishing buddy, Rodger, to a meeting at the Smokehouse Bar in early spring. It was one of his first meetings, and he was eager to learn more about the club. He was still weighing whether to join or not. Rows of chairs and a few tables were set up in the bar's shabby back room. The room has no windows, has not seen a coat of paint in many years, and can barely hold seventy-five people. The tables and many of the chairs are wobbly, there is little to no ventilation, and it smells like stale beer. Yet the club still chooses to hold meetings there. The main attraction to this meeting site is that you can order alcoholic beverages and consume them during the meeting. A few tables are set up at the front of the room for the club officers, facing the membership. To raise money painlessly, the club sells raffle tickets before each meeting for fishing tackle, and it holds a 50-50 raffle. These activities and the annual dues enable the club to sponsor tournaments, as well as to support various local fishing charities and environmental organizations.

This particular meeting's feature was a fishing guide's talk about catching salmon and other large fish in September in the Niagara River where it empties into Lake Ontario. This was his beat, and part of the purpose of his presentation was to drum up new business. Apparently, the fishing is spectacular when the fish run at that time of year.

"Just look at this!" he said as he projected slides of grinning fishermen holding up large fish they had just caught on the bar's blank wall. Even though the Niagara River was very far to go to fish, his presentation convinced me that I ought to fish there. Then the meeting's highly anticipated moment of truth arrived.

"I am now going to announce who the first place winner is in our annual winter fishing tournament," the club president boomed.

These tournaments pique the interest of many members. I have witnessed otherwise normal club members behave with ferocious competitive intensity during these tournaments, as if they were professional fisherman and finalists competing in the championship BASS masters tournament, with a $25,000 first place prize and lucrative fishing tackle company endorsements on the line. An expectant hush fell over the room.

The president grinned and paused a moment for dramatic effect. All eyes turned forward.

"Bob Wilson, come on up!" exclaimed the president with a wide smile, holding up a twelve-inch tall gold trophy cup for all to see. Everyone applauded, cheered, laughed, hooted, or booed good naturedly, as the first place winner proudly weaved his way through the maze of tables to accept the trophy.

"He must have bought the fish!" shouted one of his friends with a laugh. Bob looked at the heckler and flashed a wide smile.

After additional official business was transacted, the president cleared his throat to get everyone's attention.

"There are going to be some rule changes starting with the next fishing tournament," he announced. Suddenly the room grew quiet as the tournament junkies stopped talking (and drinking) to listen.

"Starting with the next tournament, I am not going to spend five hours at Great River Tackle, tournament headquarters, from noon until 5:00 PM, waiting for all you fishermen to come in to register your fish. We hold three tournaments a year. This is too much time for the other club officers and me to spend waiting at the tackle store. The other club officers and I have better things to do," continued the president. The statement was greeted with intense interest and dead silence in anticipation of what was coming next.

"You can all come in from 4:00 PM to 5:00 PM on tournament days to register. Shortening the registration time on tournament days will make my life so much easier," the club president concluded.

Bob Wilson, the newly anointed winner of the last tournament, sat near the front of the room, still basking in the adulation and congratulations of his fellow fishermen. Suddenly, he jumped up and started waving his arms to get the president's attention.

"You can't do that. It's not fair!" he howled.

"What do you mean, not fair, Bob?" asked the president reasonably, even though he was clearly taken aback by Bob's behavior. The room fell completely silent, and all eyes turned to witness this unusual situation.

"You have to let people come in earlier!" shouted Bob.
"No, I don't," said the president.
"It's not fair!" Bob shouted at the club president, even louder than before.
"Yes, it is fair," said the president, a little indignant at this turn of events.

By Bob's tone of voice and beet red face, it was clear that he was becoming more and more agitated. Every person in the room was riveted by the heated exchange that was rapidly escalating into confrontation.

Realizing that something was terribly wrong, the club president took a deep breath, and asked Bob in a much calmer and normal tone of voice, "Bob, why can't we run the next tournament like this?"

By this time, Bob had really worked up a head of steam. His face was purple and he neither caught, nor responded to the shift in tone and attempt by the club president to de-escalate the situation.

"Because I am getting married at 4:00 PM on that Saturday!" Bob shouted. The place went wild with laughter. Most members were laughing so hard, they were rocking back and forth in their chairs, and some were even slapping each other on the back. Rodger laughed so hard he had tears in his eyes. Bob, caught off guard by the burst of laughter, sat down. As the laughter subsided, the president stood very still, with a faraway expression on his face, deep in thought.

"OK, Bob, just this once we will make an allowance for you to come in earlier that day to get your catch registered. Is that OK?" asked the president.

Bob thought for a moment about the president's offer. By now, his complexion had lost its purple hue, and he appeared to be returning to normal.

"Yeah, that'll work," muttered Bob. The whole room erupted again with laughter.

I turned to Rodger, who was sitting next to me, and said with a grin, "I have been coming to these meetings for a long time, but this is the best fishing club meeting I ever attended. What do you think?"

"I think I'll join!" said Rodger, his mind made up.

Uncle Paul's Legacy

I believe that, next to his family, fishing was the greatest joy in my Uncle Paul's life. Paul was married to my mother's sister, Edith. Paul and Edith never had any of their own children and Paul at least partially compensated for this by taking my brother and me fishing when we were small children. The year was 1955. My brother, Del, was four and a half, and I was six years old. Paul and Edith lived only about two miles away from us. Our excitement began when Paul telephoned our house on Widener Street in Lower Baldwin, in the summer at about 5:00 PM.

"I will be there in 15 minutes, dig two dozen worms and we will go fishing tonight," was his standard line. How exited we got! We would run out back with a shovel and a can and dig frantically until he arrived. He would always warn us that if we did not dig enough worms we could not go. We always had enough worms, even if sometimes Paul had to help.

After picking us up he would drive to Nature Lodge Road near the VFW Post, and check the minnow trap he kept in Little Fishing Creek, a small stream near the town's highway bypass. He kept this trap baited and well-hidden so that no one would steal or empty it. It always had one to two dozen minnows in it. We called them shiners because of their shiny sides. We would take them with us, too.

We mostly fished the lake in front of the steel mill near Alleghoma River Dam, number four. The lake and the river were connected via a very large diameter below-the-water-level pipe. We always fished near that spot. Occasionally we fished the Alleghoma River near the old whiskey distillery – above where the Kasiwakas River, which had been polluted in the past with mine waste, empties into the Alleghoma. We never knew how Paul decided where and when to go. It was all a mystery, but we did not care as long as we were fishing.

My brother and I used cheap, off-white colored, six-foot long, fiberglass rods and open casting type reels. Edith and Paul bought these for us one Christmas. We fished with worms and bobbers, and Paul fished with minnows for bass. I had to bait my own hook, but at first, my brother could not do this, so Paul helped him. Paul grew up poor, in Kadogan on the Alleghoma River near Kitaminis. I believe that these roots biased him toward live bait fishing. He had spinning and casting rods and reels, but never a fly rod. Although we never had a conversation about it, I think he would have considered 'fly fishing' to be for 'sissies.' He was that kind of guy.

I remember that my brother caught the first fish in the family. It was about two inches long and smaller than most of the minnows Uncle Paul used as bait. We brought it home and kept in wrapped in aluminum foil in our freezer for about two months, taking it out to show anyone who came to our house. Our refrigerator was not very efficient, and the freezer did not keep the temperature much below 32°F. The longer we kept the dead fish, the worse it smelled. Eventually it smelled so bad that my mother threw it out over our strenuous objections.

My father never took us fishing, but that is another story. One summer when I was 12, my parents, my brother and I, and Aunt Edith and Uncle Paul went on vacation to Cattaraga Lake in a nearby state for a week. This was the first vacation I ever went on. There were no interstates along our route and we traveled through many small towns in the northern and less densely populated, part of our state. When we arrived on the south side of Cattaraga Lake, we found that a ferry connected the two sides of the lake at Bennis Point. There is a bridge there now, but it had not been built yet when we took this vacation. It was thrilling to take a car ferry, even when the trip took only seven minutes. The ferry moved under its own power, but actually followed a cable from one dock to the other.

We stayed near Bennis Point at Bonjour's Cabins. The cabins were old converted trolley cars near a dock on the lake. The wheels had been removed from the trolleys and their bottoms were set on a gravel base. The inside of the cabins were fairly wretched, with old oil heaters to provide warmth, an ice box (not a refrigerator), a table, some chairs and a few beds. It must have been very low-cost. This fits with the financial circumstances of my parents, and aunt and uncle. We were all very poor at the time. We used a communal shower house once a day which also housed the toilets. The owner was an old Frenchman, and we joked that the name of the place should have been, 'Excusez-moi!'

We rented a 10-foot boat and motor from a boat rental on the lake. We used this to troll for muskies. We never caught anything except vegetation, but it sure was exciting. Someone else staying at Bonjour's Cabins caught a 37-inch muskie and I watched them put the fish on a wood plank and measure it. I was fascinated. I had never seen a fish that big before in my entire life.

In my early and mid-teens I went fishing as often as I could in spring, summer, and fall. We lived on top of a 300-foot hill that overlooked the Alleghoma River, about 22 miles north of a minor metropolitan area. The street we lived on was about one block from the edge of the cliff. My brother Del and I, and my best friend David McArgyle and his younger brother Vernon, who lived about four doors up the street, would go fishing early Saturday mornings.

The only way to get to the river was by walking. We hiked down a ravine cut in the hillside by a stream. It took about 45 minutes to one hour to hike the distance. A railroad track paralleled the river along the base of the hill. A large trestle spanned the creek. We hiked under the trestle to fish the outlet of the creek into the river.

The river was several hundred yards wide at this point and all the boat traffic, which included barges, kept to a channel dredged on the far side of the river. Over the years, the creek had deposited a tongue of sand and gravel from the hillside out into the river and this served as our fishing spot. Most of the other shoreline in that area was swampy. We always had the whole area to ourselves. There was no nearby road, and the only way in and out was a long difficult hike. We never saw another fisherman at that spot. The fishing was usually pretty good. We caught bass, sunfish and anything else we could on worms. We brought canteens of water and a picnic lunch of sandwiches, and always returned home before dinnertime. It was ideal for young boys in search of adventure.

I started fly fishing in 1967 when I was 18 years old. Up until then I had a spinning outfit and a casting outfit and fished in the Alleghoma River whenever I could. I had earned some money working in construction so I bought an inexpensive Shakespeare fiberglass fly rod and automatic wind reel to have a fly fishing outfit too.

With my brand new fly rod and reel, I went fishing on opening day in April to Buffalo Creek, which had been stocked with six-inch trout by the state Fish and Game Commission. Buffalo creek flows into the Alleghoma River at Newport. I arrived before dawn. I picked a good spot and planned on fishing with salmon eggs. The stream was about 12 feet wide at that point confined between two high grassy banks.

At dawn (the official starting time for the fishing season in the state), I started fishing, caught four trout in quick succession, and returned them all to the stream. Within 20 minutes, there were four fishermen around me: two across from me on the other side of the creek, and one on either side on me on the same side of the creek. It was crowded combat fishing. They were all casting to the same spot I was. Not one of them had the decency or manners to ask permission or give me any space. Then one man waded down the center of the stream stepping on all our lines, and of course scaring all the fish.

After growing up with an entire river to fish in with no one else around, except the friends I came with, I was disgusted. I had never experienced this kind of fishing before. Nor had I heard of the term 'combat fishing.' I named these people 'water buffalo.' Supposing that fly fishing was always like this, I vowed never to go fly fishing again. I eventually gave away my fly fishing equipment.

Throughout my years at college, I only fished during the summers. But after graduation I fished almost all year round with my spinning and casting gear. I fished with friends and sometimes alone from shore on lakes, ponds, and rivers in the state where I lived, and occasionally took trips to several surrounding states. By this time in my life, my Uncle Paul had moved to the east coast of Florida, where he became a dedicated Snook enthusiast. We would call each other from time to time, and tell the other about our latest fishing adventures. We always inserted tall tales among the mostly true stories. And concluded each phone call with laughter, with mutual promises to call again. Each conversation was a gem, and I remember them with pleasure.

In early spring 1978, I took my son on his first fishing trip. We went to a pond in the woods off Stake Road in the town where we lived. He was four years old and had his own rod, reel and fishing hat. He caught a four-inch long sunfish. We still have the picture of his first triumph. The pond was about two miles from our house and about one-quarter mile from Stake Road, down a dirt road through a wood. It was not possible to drive down this road because there was an old chain fastened across it, about 10 yards into the wood. A car could park there, however. The pond, road, and wood have since disappeared, replaced by a housing development. I mourned this loss of habitat.

In the spring of 1991, my daughter was scheduled to go to 6th grade camp. One of the camp activities listed was fishing. My daughter told me that she thought that she wanted to try this, and I felt guilty that I had never taken her fishing. In my defense, she was not interested in what she considered to be a predominately male activity, no matter how many times I asked her to go. I didn't want her to go to camp without some fishing knowledge, skills, and experience. Classmates can be very unforgiving when you are in 6th grade.

So one gray, cloudy day in late April, I took her to Growltown Lakes in the county park system. We bought red worms nearby and went in search of blue gills. We fished early one Saturday morning. Last year's cattail stocks and some algae surrounded the lake which made it hard to approach open water. We found a spot, and I showed her how to put a bobber, hook and sinker on the line. I put the worm on the hook, as she was too squeamish to do this by herself, and explained the rudiments of bobber fishing. I told her about being patient and waiting for the bobber to be pulled under before setting the hook. She caught a few blue gills that day and I took her picture with her first fish. She was thrilled. Eventually, she became one of my best fly fishing buddies. A father's love and patience won the day.

As my children grew, their interest in fishing waxed and waned as they went through various phases of their life.

In 1995, John Barnheart, an accountant at a company where I was working, was treasurer of the Central Lakes Fishing Association (CLFA) at that time. He persuaded me to try fly fishing again and attend my first meeting of this fishing club. At that meeting, the main speaker presented a slide show, and discussed how, when, and where to fish for 'big' bass. He also showed how to tie some bass flies. I was hooked. (Pun intended.) At the first few CLFA meetings I attended, the members of the club taught me how to tie some common flies, and how to present a fly to catch a trout. My earliest fly patterns for trout flies were taught to me by Ken Mankowski, the club education officer, who has since passed away. He was a great teacher, fun, patient and encouraging. I then bought a fly tying book, the first of many.

When I first started fly fishing, I fished all seasons in a large nearby river and in creeks that emptied into it. In the winter, the temperature was so cold sometimes that ice would freeze in my rod guides. I no longer fish under these conditions, and wait until the temperature is at least above freezing. I ignore most other weather conditions, and try to go when the fish are biting. I usually call a fly fishing store near where I want to fish and ask for stream conditions. Then I decide whether to go or not. I also have friends that I call for advice on stream conditions and whether the fish are biting.

I started keeping a journal to preserve some technical information about fishing trips and tackle, but at some point, it changed to include preserving memories of a lifetime of fishing. The information I was initially preserving was how to tie various flies, records of fishing trips including dates, where we went, weather and stream conditions, what was caught and on what flies. I also recorded who went and any other brief thoughts. After a while, I realized that reading these notes about old trips helped me remember them and let me relive some good times. This journal was, in fact, preserving memories. I have continued writing in my journal for many years now and have shared them as stories with my family, close friends, and now in this collection of short stories.

About 2004, my Uncle Paul was living in Coca Beach, Florida, with his second wife and their young child, and he was battling cancer. At one especially low point near the end of his illness, I helped dispel his depression and rally his courage by talking with him about our old fishing times and suggesting future ones with his baby daughter. Shortly thereafter, he lost his fight and passed away. After the funeral, his wife thanked me very much for what I did for him. Actually, I realized that it was the other way around, and what he had done for me. And told her so.

Looking back, I can clearly see that my passion for fishing is a legacy handed down to me from Uncle Paul, and many others throughout my life, who took the time to share with me their passion and love of fishing. With this in mind, I consider what my own legacy will be. I feel obligated, humbled, and honored to show and tell the next several generations what I love about the sport of fishing. How can I, or really any of us who love fishing, do less?

The Catch of the Day

A regional Wildlife Officer from the state Department of Natural Resources (DNR) spoke for a few minutes at a recent meeting of a local fishing club. My friend and fishing buddy, Rodger, and I attended. The officer was intelligent, knowledgeable, and came across as a classy guy. He studiously ignored the verbal suggestions that DNR stood for 'Do Not Resuscitate.' I am sure he was on the receiving end of this jibe many times before from groups of fishermen. The officer talked about the abundance of gamefish in our state and then opened up the floor for questions.

"Are there any questions I can answer for you?" he concluded. I think he was expecting questions about stocking locations, number of fish stocked, stocking dates, stream access, or current fishing conditions.

"Can you tell us about any recent criminal activity?" was a prompt first question.

"Whoa!" said Rodger in surprise. "That's not what I expected." I was surprised, as well, and could tell from the expressions on their faces that most of the members were surprised, too. I wondered how many questions the officer was going to be asked that night about criminal activity.

All eyes turned toward the officer as the room fell silent. He paused for a moment, smiled and began to recount a tale of technology, criminal activity and international intrigue. Heady stuff for a local fishing club meeting. He started to talk, hesitant at first and then smoother and faster as the story began to take shape.

On Christmas Day, a Connaught Falls man and his good friend, visiting from France, went fishing for trout. They caught many trout using a net. Apparently eating fresh caught fish is part of a traditional French holiday feast. They also video-recorded their activities and put the whole experience on YouTube.com. Shortly thereafter, complaints started coming in to the Fish and Wildlife Division of the DNR about this. Some callers claimed that they recognized the terrain as being somewhere in our state. The division could not continue to ignore these complaints without investigating, but access to the YouTube website is blocked on state computers. Finally, one officer went home, downloaded the offensive video to his flash drive, and brought it back to work.

Back at the office, numerous officials viewed the file. Decisions were made, and copies of this video were sent to all district enforcement officers. When our speaker viewed the video, he quickly recognized where the video was taken (it was in his jurisdiction) and shortly thereafter who it was. He served the Connaught Falls man with a warrant. His friend had since gone back to France. The Frenchman was clearly beyond the reach of the DNR, and could not be extradited for such a misdemeanor. However, with an outstanding warrant, the Frenchman could not get back in the country. They both hired the same attorney to represent them. Charges included one count of trout fishing with a net (illegal), fishing without a license (illegal) and taking more than the daily species limit (illegal).

The trial before a judge was speedy, as the evidence was overwhelming. They were quickly found guilty in spite of the efforts of their lawyer. The Frenchman did not have to appear personally, but paid $200 in fines though their attorney. The Connaught Falls man paid $500. The Frenchman is now free to return to the United States anytime he wants fresh trout, with a valid fishing license obviously.

"If they had just caught a few fish with their bare hands there would have been no charges!" I told Rodger with a laugh.

"Or if they hadn't videotaped themselves committing the crime, or hadn't put it on the internet," responded Rodger, shaking his head in disbelief.

"Any more questions?" asked the officer, hoping for something more ordinary, I'm sure. But by this time, criminal activity was fixed in the minds of the membership. A hand shot up in the second row.

"Yes," said the officer pointing to the hand in the air. The hand belonged to Joe Bob and everyone in the club knew him. Joe Bob was one of those people who had a reputation for knowing secret fishing hot spots, catching a lot of big fish, and for pushing the rules just a little.

"Has anyone ever been arrested for trespassing while fishing on private property?" asked Joe Bob. The room became instantly quiet. For some reason, this was of very great interest to the majority of the fishermen present at the meeting. Not that anyone present would ever stoop to doing something like this.

"Yes, just last year," was the answer. "A certain fisherman was fishing for steelhead on posted private property," said the officer. "The owner asked him to leave. The fisherman refused to leave, and furthermore was belligerent to the landowner. The fisherman may have been intoxicated but there was no direct proof. The many empty crushed beer cans on the owner's property found near the fisherman could have been put there by anyone, or even washed downstream by the current. The owner called the county sheriff's office. A patrol car came to the property and the sheriff's deputy found the fisherman still on the stream. In addition to trespassing, the perpetrator did not have a fishing license, and was over the daily limit," concluded the officer.

"How much did it cost him?" asked Joe Bob.

"$200," was the answer. "Why do you ask?"

"Oh, I just wanted to know if it was worth it or not," Joe Bob responded with a grin, as the club membership laughed with delight.

Lake Okeechobee Fishing

On a semester break from the university I was attending, I visited my parents who had moved to Vero Beach, Florida. My Uncle Paul and Aunt Edith were also visiting my mom and dad at the same time. Paul and Edith lived in a cold northern state and drove to Florida for a warmer winter vacation. My uncle was an avid fisherman and brought his fishing equipment with him. My father didn't own any fishing equipment. Paul couldn't fish anywhere near his house in January with the expectation of catching anything at his usual spots on the river that was his home water. I know that he wanted to get some fishing time in on his vacation. So one morning, Uncle Paul, my father and I went to Lake Okeechobee to do some bass fishing.

I am sure that this particular trip was my uncle's idea. My brother, Del, was not with us as he was attending college in Wisconsin at the time. None of us had ever been to Lake Okeechobee before and had no idea how large it really was. When we got to the lake, we saw that there was no real possibility of shore fishing and that a boat was needed. The day was gray and overcast, and not too warm. Winter temperatures vary a lot from day to day in Florida in the winter. We traveled the roads around the lake until we found a marina in a small cove where we rented a 10-foot boat with a small motor. The boat looked too small to carry three people, a motor and gas, but as my uncle and father were paying and making all the decisions, I was in no position to judge or make recommendations.

"What could go wrong?" Paul asked out loud to no one in particular, as if in response to my thought.

"There are alligators in the swamps around here and the lake, too, so try not to go swimming," replied the marina dock hand, who was helping us make the boat ready. "Just be careful and watch out for them. I don't think that they'll bother you," he added. I then mentally compared the length of an imagined adult alligator to the length of our boat. The comparison was not favorable.

The dock hand topped off the gas tank and we left the dock. We guided the boat along the shore of the cove. Lake Okeechobee, about 30 miles wide east-west and 35 miles long north-south, was too large to take a small boat very far from shore. Anyway, as I was helping load the boat, the marina proprietor gave Paul directions on where to fish. We aimed for a spot about half way around the cove from the marina, in shallow water by some tall water weeds. Paul guided the boat. He turned off the motor and let the boat drift the final 10 yards to the spot he had picked so as not to disturb the fish. Following directions he received, Paul, judged that if we anchored the boat about 10 yards from shore and cast towards the weeds we would have some luck.

As we began to fish, a slight wind began to blow. We found ourselves drifting closer to the weeds. Our anchor was dragging. At first, this actually let us cast on either side of the boat to cover more water close to the weeds with our casts. Finally, my uncle decided that we were too close to the weeds and needed to reposition the boat. He got out the oars to try to move us silently and stealthily. Just as he fitted the oars into the oarlocks, we were shocked by loud screeching.

Up to that point the only sounds we heard were small ones. But this sounded like the volume you would expect with a jet engine taking off, more than 100 decibels. A heron had been silently and motionlessly standing in the weeds only a few yards away watching us. His blue gray coloring blended into his background so perfectly, and he was so still, we had not noticed him. After the loud cry, he jumped out of the water and began flapping his wings, making a beeline straight toward us.

We all instinctively ducked. He flew over us, just missing the gunwales of the boat by about 12 inches. We thought we were being attacked, but soon realized that the weeds were too tall for him to fly in any other direction. He needed a long expanse of water to gain speed and altitude. He was a large bird and his wingspan seemed to me to be wider than our boat was long. I was scared for a few seconds, but afterward we all laughed. We caught a few bass on this trip, but it was the close encounter with the heron that I fondly remember.

My First (and So Far Only) Deep Sea Fishing Trip

I am primarily a freshwater fisherman, and have been all my life. However, in the summer of 1970, I was working in Boca Raton, Florida, as a summer intern at a research laboratory. This job was between my junior and senior years at the university where I was studying electrical engineering. My summer job was to help design the next generation large-scale computer. I earned $650 per month. This was a princely sum in those days for a summer intern. I lived in an apartment right on the beach that I shared with another company intern to minimize living expenses. There were always parties Friday and Saturday nights, attended by almost all the company interns and other young professionals. I was 21, unattached, and there were young girls in bathing suits everywhere. Life was good.

The group of older engineers that I was working with were planning to go on a deep sea sport fishing charter trip that summer. They had five anglers signed up, but needed one more. I quickly volunteered to be the sixth. I think that my share of the expenses was $50. This was for a half-day cruise.

We arrived at the dock early in the morning, and I saw the charter boat for the first time. It looked huge. The boat was docked at an inlet marina near Pompano Beach, a town south of Boca Raton on the Atlantic coast.

As the charter boat pulled out of the inlet and headed straight out into the Atlantic to get to the Gulf Stream where we were to do our fishing, the bottoms of the high rise buildings disappeared over the horizon first, then their middles and then their tops. As soon as the last building top disappeared, I realized how small the boat was compared to the size of the ocean. I felt like we were a small bobbing cork!

The boat had only two fighting chairs. These seats were large swivel chairs firmly bolted to the deck facing the stern. The person doing the fishing was strapped into the chair and the rod was attached to a leather pocket in the lap of the fisherman and also tethered to the chair. The fishing lines went up to a pulley at a height of about seven feet, and angled at about 45 degrees down and out, toward the side of the boat. When it was my turn, I was given heavy leather gloves to hold the rod. In the event of a strike, I was instructed to jerk the rod up hard three times to set the hook. The hooks were enormous and held what looked to be a two-pound slice of raw fish. We fished by trawling at about 3-5 knots in the Gulf Stream.

It was a nice sunny summer day and we cruised back and forth. The temperature was warm but not hot. The sky was sprinkled with big fluffy white clouds, the winds were light and the swells were less than two feet. I could tell that we were occasionally making turns, by the shape of the wake, but without a fixed reference or access to a compass, I could not tell what pattern we were following, if any.

We took turns sitting in the chairs and fishing. When I wasn't sitting in a chair, I wandered around the boat. The captain was piloting the boat from the flying bridge, comprised of a chair and a wheel covered by a canvas awning, on the roof of the real pilot house. In the real pilot house, the wheel mimicked what the pilot was doing. Over the wheel was a brass plaque entitled "The Seaman's Prayer." The prayer read, "O God, Your ocean is so large, and my boat is so small." I knew exactly how that seaman felt!

During the trip, I caught a 48" male bonito. It was pretty exciting, and took me more than 20 minutes to reel him in. The fish was thrown into the fish locker. When a crew member asked me if I wanted to take it home and eat it, I said no. The crew then cut it up for bait. Several of the other engineers caught fish too. More than 40 years later, this is still the largest fish I ever caught.

Canoe Adventures

I own a canoe and keep the registration current. I had always wanted a canoe but could never afford to buy one. With two children and a house in the suburbs, there was always something we needed to purchase more urgently. A canoe seemed frivolous. Then in 1993, the Vice President of Engineering and my boss at the company where I was working got himself fired. He lived in a nearby town. Within a few months of his termination, he called me to say that he had a new job and was leaving town for the Southwest.

"I am going to be doing consulting and teaching at a state university," he said. "I own a 17-foot Grumman aluminum canoe built in 1970, and its load rating is 1,500 pounds. The price is free, but if you want it, you have to come and cart it away since I am not going to pay to move it."

"Do you want it?" he asked.

"I will be right over," I replied.

When I inspected the canoe, I discovered that it had been stored under a tree in his backyard for more than a dozen years. It was very dirty and the aluminum hull showed stains from dead leaves, pools of water that had accumulated from rain and snow, bird droppings, and tree sap. It had no registration. Its biggest defect was a hole in the bottom near the keel. I pointed this out when I saw it.

"Yes, we landed on a rock," he said. "My family hasn't used it since."

"Do you still want it, now that you have seen it?" he asked.

"Yes," I said. "I know that I can fix the hole and make it watertight again. I will be back within a week to pick it up." My former boss was very pleased. He was tight with a dollar and did not want to have to pay someone to take it away.

Coincidentally, I was planning to rent a truck within a few weeks, to help with the closing of my mother-in-law's apartment. I decided that I would also use it to bring the canoe to my house.

Bringing the canoe to my house was no problem with the rental truck. I spent many hours cleaning the canoe inside and out and patched the hole with a plastic compound that required a plumber's propane torch to heat and fuse the sealing material around the aluminum. The patch worked and has held ever since. I registered the canoe with the State Department of Natural Resources. A three-year license costs only $15. I was a proud owner of a canoe. It was too big to keep in my garage, so I had to keep it outside behind the house. I selected a spot near the rear of our property. I built two wooden sawhorses, and store the canoe upside down on them. Occasionally, it blows over in a very strong wind, and I have to upright it again.

Using the canoe showed its good and bad qualities. The wide flat bottom provided for a very large load carrying capacity. The canoe actually rides better with a heavy load. With the flat bottom, a light load and a cross wind is all that it takes to blow the canoe all over the surface of a body of water. The canoe has no real keel to keep us on our course.

The canoe received heavy usage on multiple Boy Scout trips. When the other scouts were using rental canoes I cautioned care around rocks or if their canoes scraped on underwater obstructions. As soon it was my canoe they were using, I found myself getting nervous and hollering at the boys.

"Don't hit those rocks! Be careful," I would yell, when they were near some natural obstruction in the stream.

My daughter and I made it into the 1998 Edition of the Guinness Book of World Records (page 626) with this canoe. The entry reads, "A raft of 582 kayaks and canoes, organized by the Metroparks, was held together by hands only for 30 seconds while free floating on Hinkley Lake, on May 21, 1995." A picture of the "raft" was also shown. My daughter and I are in the photo, but we cannot be individually distinguished among all the other canoes. Afterward we accidentally tipped over and got wet, discovering that Hinkley Lake is not very deep. It was fun anyway.

On one fine summer day in 1999, my son and I took the canoe fly fishing on the East Branch of the Cayuga River, near Bunton. We put in at Kinsmen Road and paddled to Taveras Road (a distance of 0.7 miles) and back again. The path of the river formed the hypotenuse of a triangle with the main roads. We were able to reach sections of the stream that were inaccessible by land and could only be fished from a boat. The stream went through cow pastures and marshes and dense woods. We saw many fish jumping and caught a few bass on popper flies. We tried all the nymph and dry patterns I had brought along, but only the poppers worked. The stream was very beautiful and secluded in this section. Civilization seemed very far away at times. We both had a very good time.

I have only used the canoe sparingly for fishing trips since then but intend to do many more when my grandchildren get older. Since it only costs $5 per year to keep it registered and costs nothing to operate, the price is right. It is not hurting anything by sitting in my back yard. I tease my wife that, someday when the creek near our house overflows, I'll use it to rescue us and all the neighbors. I hope that this is an idle jest.

At some point in time, I intend to give my canoe to one of my grandchildren, preferably one who shows a real interest in scouting or fishing.

Fly Fishing the Yellowstone River

In August of 1996, my son planned to travel to Palo Alto, California, to attend graduate school. He needed to drive, so he could take almost all his worldly possessions, and to have a car when he got there. At the time, he was driving a 1988 Honda Accord that we purchased used from our family car mechanic. I had bought him this car and put several hundred dollars of repairs in it so that it could even make the trip. He asked several of his friends to help him drive across the United States to California, but since they had just graduated with bachelor's' degrees and started new jobs, or were going to graduate school themselves, none of his friends could help him. Finally, he asked me. We joked that I was his last choice.

"Sure, but under two conditions," I answered. "We have to stop at Yellowstone National Park and fly fish and we have to stop at Yosemite to sightsee for a day." He hugged me and said in apparent agreement, "These are conditions?"

I immediately bought my return airline ticket and started tying useful fly patterns. I wasn't very experienced in tying flies at that time, only just having started, but wanted to do a good job, so I bought a book, "Fly Patterns of Yellowstone." I also went to the local automobile association office no less than three times, getting maps, pouring over them, to trim our route in time and distance. I also kept calling the Yellowstone Park travel service daily, trying to book a room at the Yellowstone Lodge for the night we needed. This lodge is 100% booked up to a year in advance, so my frequent calls were to try to get a room from a cancellation. Fortunately, this strategy worked and two weeks before we left, we had a room at the lodge. I went to the local National Recreation Area and bought an annual National Park pass so that we would not have to waste time waiting in lines to buy individual passes on our trip.

So on August 8th we set off at 5:00 AM from our hometown to drive to Yellowstone and points farther west. On our first day, we drove 14 hours and made it to Omaha, Nebraska. On our second day we made it to Wind River, Wyoming.

On our third day, as we were approaching the Continental Divide, we would come around a curve in the road and see a spectacular view, my son would ask, "Are those mountains yet?" and I kept saying no, not yet. This happened several, if not many, times. When finally we first glimpsed the Continental Divide, I finally said "Yes!" We stopped at the highest part of the pass over the divide to look around. We arrived at Yellowstone about noon and entered the park with our pass, bypassing the 'purchase' line of about 20 cars and the associated delay.

We toured the park, saw Old Faithful, Norris Basin, hot springs, bubbling mud, other geysers, buffalo, elk, the waterfalls and the river gorge, registered at the lodge, bought our fishing licenses, and after dinner at the lodge decided to go fly fishing. Earlier that day when we drove past the Yellowstone River, we noticed signs saying "No Fishing" in the part of the river closest to Yellowstone Lake, where fish were spawning. We didn't think much of it at the time.

We noticed that almost all the trees are small and stunted in Yellowstone due to the short growing season. Also, there was a large fire in Yellowstone in 1988, a few years before our visit. In the burned areas, we saw the fire damaged trees that were still standing (black trunks) and new small trees that were growing where the sun now touched the ground.

That evening, as we drove north from the Fishing Bridge area near Yellowstone Lake, we saw tens of thousands of rise rings in the Yellowstone River from trout feeding on surface insects. We were thrilled beyond belief. The river surface was covered with overlapping rings. This was a higher density of fish than we ever could have imagined!

Naturally, this was the posted area we had seen earlier, and fishing was off limits in this section of the river. No matter, we would fish just above the posted section. Fish can't read. The fishing promised to be great. When we got to the non-posted section of the river, parked and went down the bank to the stream, we were disappointed. There were no "rise rings." Not even one! How can the fish know this? We tried every fly we had, both dry and wet, with no strikes and no indication that fish had ever been in this river. We were disappointed but decided to come back and fish the next morning.

At dark, as we were loading the car with our fishing gear, I laid my fly vest on the back hood of the car while I was getting out of my waders. But by then dusk had turned to night and I forgot that the vest was there as we drove off without noticing. When we got to the lodge I realized what I had done. We went back to the spot where we had parked and looked. The elapsed time was only about 15 minutes, but the damage was done. We could not find the vest. My name was in the vest so I hoped that some honest tourist would turn it in. Luckily, I still had some flies and all my other gear so we could fish the following morning.

We discovered that there were no televisions or radios in the rooms or common areas and there was no radio reception on our car radio either. Yellowstone Lake is virtually surrounded by a ring of mountains 11,000 feet tall. This was a good reason for no AM or FM radio station reception.

My son had a trout for dinner. We joked that this was probably going to be the only trout we encountered on the whole trip.

Evening entertainment was provided by a string quartet in the common room wearing tuxedoes playing classical music. The lodge was quaint, and it felt like we were transported back to the early 1900s. We got up at dawn and fished until 9:00 AM, only catching one Lake Trout between us. But our reward was the sun coming up over the snow-capped mountains while we fished a really beautiful stream. I know that we had a good spot on the water, because all morning other fisherman came to try the spot, only to discover that we were there first. It would be two more years before I caught my first cutthroat trout.

We visited the ranger stations, asking if anyone had turned in a vest. With only negative responses, I left my name and number in case anyone would still turn the vest in. I never did recover the vest. I am not upset over the loss of the vest. I replaced it with a much better one. The loss that was really hard to take was the hundred flies that were in the vest in small plastic boxes, all of which I had tied myself. I hope that whoever found the vest enjoyed the use of the flies.

After fishing in the morning, we went back to the lodge to shower and have breakfast. We were served breakfast by a college-age girl working there for the summer. We were remarking to ourselves how beautiful everything was and I was saying that I wanted to buy a house and retire here. The waitress heard us and said, "Yes, it is nice around here. The ice breaks on the lake about June 6th." I thought, "Wait a minute."

"If the ice breaks on the lake on June 6th, when does it start snowing?" I asked her.

"It starts snowing the second week of September," she responded. Counting in my head, I thought, "Holy cow, if that is true then there is only 10 weeks of spring, summer and fall, and 42 weeks of winter each year." I asked her if this was true.

"You're right," she said. "We are at 8,000 feet of altitude on the Continental Divide, pretty far north (latitude), so what did you expect?" Right then I decided that I would not retire here.

We left Yellowstone and toured Grand Teton National Park before heading to Idaho and points beyond. That night we stayed in Idaho Falls, Idaho. We got up very early the next day and were determined to cross the Nevada desert before the heat of the day. We were doing better than 80 miles an hour on the interstate but the locals were passing us as if we were standing still. We were scheduled to spend the night in Reno, but we arrived there at about 2:00 PM. We considered that this was too early to stop, so we made reservations for Bridgeport, California, and cancelled our reservations in Reno. Bridgeport is just on the east side of Tioga Pass, which goes over the Sierra Nevada Mountains near Yosemite National Park.

When we arrived at Bridgeport, we discovered that there was a gas station, a restaurant, a post office/general store, two motels and five fly fishing stores. It turns out that Bridgeport is the Mecca of fly fishing on the eastern slope of the Sierra Nevada Mountains. We didn't know this when we pulled into town.

We visited all the fly shops and learned what we could in case we ever came back that way again. I later bought a book that describes the fishing in this area. At dinner that night, a chain gang of prisoners came in to the restaurant where we were eating. It was very dry in that part of the country that summer. There were signs everywhere that said that the danger of fire was high. Apparently, they had been doing firefighting.

The deputy sheriffs had large looking guns. The place had an old red horizontal Coca Cola cooler with lots of bottles of Coke in it. The jukebox only played country and western music. It was the only kind of music we could get on the car radio for days.

On our way out of Bridgeport, we passed Mono Lake, where strange rock formations were exposed when the water level dropped. We saw that environmentalists had put up signs that said, "Save Mono Lake." The next day we drove over the pass and saw a wonderful view of Yosemite from the backside. It was quite a sight. We toured Yosemite and drove into Palo Alto that evening. We had driven just over 3,000 miles. We drove it in 50 hours (moving), with an average of over 60 miles per hour.

My son moved in to start his five-year stay at graduate school. On our last night together in San Francisco, he and I had dinner at The Mandarin Restaurant, one of my favorites. I felt that we had forged a bond through six days of travel across the continent and through all our adventures. I knew that, henceforth, for the rest of our lives I was only going to see him infrequently. With these thoughts in mind, I cried in the restaurant as I was trying to give him some fatherly advice that he really did not need. I told him that I loved him and that he had made me so proud. I told him to do well at graduate school, stay true to himself, and "Follow your destiny." During my teary monolog he just kept grinning and saying, "There, there, Dad." Maybe someday he will be fortunate enough to be in my shoes and experience a moment like this.

More than twenty years later, we still fondly remember this trip.

Rocky Mountain National Park

In the summer of 1998, I started working for a new company. That fall a National Laboratory in Golden, Colorado, sponsored a technical conference. My first business trip with this company was to attend this conference. The meeting was held in Denver at a downtown hotel near the Denver Mint. The meeting started on a Monday, but I arranged to fly out Saturday morning instead of Sunday to save on airfare.

Alex, my son's undergraduate college roommate, was working for a Fortune 500 electronics company, and living in Fort Collins, Colorado. Fort Collins is only 55 miles due north of Denver. At the time, my son was doing postgraduate work in Palo Alto, California. He had received his Master's degree in June of 1998 and had elected to stay on for his PhD.

I wanted to use this business trip as an opportunity to fly fish in Rocky Mountain National Park (RMNP), but my wife would only agree to this expedition under the condition that I take someone with me. Since I'd never been there before, this seemed a prudent thing for me to do. So I called Alex and he immediately agreed to accompany me on that Sunday. I called ahead to a local fishing store and they encouraged me to come. Alex and I were to meet at 10:00 AM at the fly-fishing store in Estes Park, Colorado. Estes Park, elevation 7,500 feet, is the city at the main entrance to RMNP. It is about 64 miles northwest of Denver and 30 miles southwest of Fort Collins.

I was very excited for my fishing expedition to the RMNP and I made sure I was on time to meet Alex. I walked into the fishing store and to my absolute astonishment, my son was in the store with Alex. He had flown in from San Francisco the day before and had stayed at Alex's house the previous night. My son and I hugged each other with tears in our eyes. I was not expecting to see him until three months later at

Christmas, so it was a little emotional for me. I cherish all father-son time we spend together.

"I wanted to surprise you, Dad," he explained.

"Wow, you sure did!" I replied.

After greeting Alex and recovering from my heartwarming reception, I asked the store manager for a few suggestions and directions to a good fly-fishing spot.

"How much physical exercise are you boys willing to experience to get to the fishing spot?" he asked.

"We're all in pretty good shape," I said.

"How much time do you have?" he asked.

"All day, but today only, I have to drive to Denver tonight," I replied.

"What do you want to catch?" he asked.

"Cutthroat trout," I quickly responded.

"Then you should go to Sky Pond," he replied. "You can get directions from the rangers at the visitors' center."

"Thanks very much," I said.

"What will the trout bite on at Sky Pond?" I asked. He then showed me some flies that he said would work well for us. Before we left the store, I looked it over for anything else that we might need, purchased the flies, and a few other items.

We then headed out to the park entrance, leaving Alex's car in the store's parking lot. When we arrived at the park's visitor center, I bought a good topographical map of the park. Like all adventurous anglers, I keep a high quality compass in my fishing vest at all times. Having taught orienteering to the Boy Scouts on my son's camping trips, I was confident in my skill to help us find the way to Sky Pond. After all, the ranger said the trail was marked, so navigating a drive to the trailhead and hiking to Sky Pond did not appear to be very difficult.

Perfect weather conditions awaited us. The sun was shining, the sky was blue, and the temperature appeared to be about 50°F. The weather forecast for that day was for mild temperatures and clear skies. This was important as the weather is notoriously changeable in RMNP and it had recently snowed. Amazingly, it can snow any day of the year in the park!

We drove from the visitor's center to Bear Lake, elevation 9,500 feet, where we parked the car. We then hiked about four miles to Sky Pond (elevation 10,850 feet) using my compass and the "topo" map I had purchased. There was a rugged path apparently dubbed a trail, so with the combination of the trail markers, "topo" characteristics, and a compass heading we had enough information to make the hike without a problem. This four-mile horizontal distance took us 2½ hours of constant climbing up 1,350 vertical feet.

The views of the mountains on the trail were breathtaking! The trail passed near a 25-foot high thunderous waterfall that cascaded down with such volume that you knew it was birthed from the sun shining on high mountain snowfields. The entire trail was steep. Some of the trail was alongside a very steep mountainside; some of it was along a water channel made by Glacier Creek and the last few hundred yards, in a valley formed by Icy Creek, the outlet of the lake. I could tell from hiking up the mountain that the air was thinner than I was used to. In front of us was a mountain called the Shark's Tooth. Its elevation is 12,680 feet. To the right of us was Tyndall Glacier and to the left of us was Taylor Glacier whose melt ran into a creek that fed Sky Pond. Seeing glaciers this close made us feel like we were in the presence of one of God's creations.   The lake was just at the elevation of the tree line at that latitude. It looked to be about 10 acres in size.

When we arrived at the lake we ate the lunch we had brought. Having approached Sky Pond from the direction of the outlet stream, we then had to circle the lake until we came to the creek that fed it. Providence smiled upon us as we gazed on about a dozen cutthroat trout just inside the stream mouth waiting for insects that the stream would deliver to them. There was snow on the ground in the shadows. It had already snowed at this elevation even though it was the middle of October. The lake had some ice on it near the outlet; however, it was thin and did not cover more than a small portion of the lake.

I put on my fishing waders and vest that I had carried up the trail in my backpack. I brought a four-weight seven-piece travel rod and a matching reel with me. I assembled the rod and reel, and looked around for any flies that might be in the air so I would know what the fish might be feeding on. I did not immediately see any, but the trout seemed to be taking small gray flies off the surface. I knelt down in the snow so as not to be seen by the trout and floated a small dry Adams fly over them. I tried this several times with no effect.

"What else should I do?" I asked my son.

"Why don't you try wiggling the fly a little on the surface film? Move them sort of like the real ones are moving?" he suggested.

I turned to my son and asked, "Like this?" as I put several small twitches on the line, causing the fly to skitter across the surface.

A fifteen-inch cutthroat hit the fly while I was not looking. Instinctively, I set the hook by feel. After he felt my line, he ran out into the lake. I played him carefully so as not to disturb the other fish. When I landed him, he was beautifully marked with a reddish orange gash under his mouth. I had caught my first cutthroat trout! I could not resist the photo opportunity with my first catch, and after taking his picture, I quickly released him. I then caught another one with the same method, and released him too. This time the struggle spooked the other fish and they all swam out into the lake. The lake was crystal clear so visibility was no problem. We stood on a large boulder near the inlet stream and cast to them in the lake with no further strikes of any kind. Unfortunately, the fish had been spooked and were now very wary.

The cutthroat trout is a beautiful specimen. It is silvery, brassy, and black-spotted with an almost fluorescent red color at the gill covers (which looks like the throat area) hence the common name.

After an hour or so with no further luck, we had to leave Sky Pond to be back at the car before dark. None of us wanted to be on a dangerously steep mountain trail in the dark and it was a 2½-hour hike. As we were leaving the pond, I had to cross the inlet stream and misjudged the depth of it because the water was so crystal clear. I fell completely forward into the near freezing water. I quickly recovered but all my clothes were wet. Fortunately, for my internal body temperature, the air temperature was still above freezing, but the shadows were beginning to lengthen and ominously we could tell that the temperature was rapidly falling. In order to avoid hypothermia on the way down the mountain, my son immediately had me undress and Alex and my son each gave me one or two pieces of their dry clothes. This worked to keep me warm during the descent to the Bear Lake parking lot.

That evening I took my son and Alex to a good Italian restaurant before leaving them at Alex's car. It was a big surprise to see my son and it was a great fishing day too. It was tough saying goodbye to my son after only spending a few hours with him, but those few hours I will cherish forever. I had a high altitude adventure with my son and I had caught my first (and second) cutthroat trout.

Catching (and releasing) a cutthroat trout was very important to me. Before the "white man" came to what we now call "The West," the habitat of the cutthroat was vast, extending to all of Wyoming, Colorado, and eastern Montana throughout the entire Yellowstone River drainage, up to the Missouri River. Apparently, the Missouri was too muddy for the species. In the 1880s, brook trout and brown trout were introduced from the East into most of these areas and they drove out all the cutthroat trout. The habitat of the cutthroat trout is now very limited, so catching one is a very special event. I hope that more of their habitat can be restored to them in the future. They are a very beautiful fish and should be more widely available for more anglers to enjoy. Although, given their rarity, I am happy to have some bragging rights that I caught and released a cutthroat trout.

Twilight Catch

It was late June, and my son, my friend Alan, and I were fishing Spring Creek near Fisherman's Paradise. I love fishing with my son, and Alan is a good friend and a good fly fisherman, who also happens to be a minister. While this combination put some limitations on my vocabulary, not to mention the stories I could tell about the size of the fish that got away, each of them was fun to be with and great fishing partners, too. On this trip, we stayed at a nearby bed and breakfast in Bellefonte that catered to fly fishermen. The weather was perfect … lofty cirrus clouds and high temperatures in the lower 70s. We fished that day at two other nearby streams, and ended up at Spring Creek after dinner.

On this particular trip, we targeted streams in mountain valleys in the Appalachians. The mountains in this part of the state are lovely in the summer, covered in rich green forests. The ridges extend almost directly north-south with steep sided valleys in between. In some of these valleys run world-class trout streams. At the bottom of the valleys, the sun disappears early behind the mountain ridge to the west, giving the effect of a long lingering twilight. It was about 9:00 PM, a cloudless evening with no wind. The sky overhead was far brighter than the light in the valley, which was slowly fading. It was very quiet and peaceful with only the sound of water rushing over small stones to break the silence.

I had just caught a twelve-inch brown trout on a #18 Light Cahill fly that I had tied a few days prior to our trip. The fish put up a fight and I had no net to land him, having lent it to my son earlier in the day. I took him to the shore to remove the fly and release him. This fly closely resembled the tiny white flies that were congregating over the surface of the water. It wasn't exactly a hatch, but numerous flies hovered over the stream. The flies were flitting very fast in seemingly random patterns. My chewed fly still looked reasonably intact, so I decided to keep using it. Besides, the light in the valley was almost gone, and it would have been difficult to tie on a new fly under those conditions. I wanted to spend my remaining time on the stream trying a few more casts before we had to leave.

I carefully waded out into the stream and began casting. Suddenly, mid-cast, more than a dozen bats appeared from beyond the treetops. They flew down close to me swooping after the insects. I thought that the white flies were fast, but the bats' speed made the flies look lethargic! I continued to cast, and a bat dived after my fly. I was startled at the spectacle, but impressed that it could swoop down and like lightning close the distance on my speeding fly. At the last possible moment, the bat veered off.

"Thank goodness!" I thought, relieved that this bat recognized that the fly was not a meal. Maybe it noticed the fly line or the hook with its radar when it got close enough. As I continued casting this bat-fly chase happened about a dozen times, each with the bat pulling out of its dive at the last possible moment.

"I wish the trout were attracted to my flies like these bats are," was my next thought.

After many aerial chase scenes with no result, I realized that the bats were smart enough not to eat an imitation insect attached to a line. I concluded that I could safely ignore the bat situation and concentrate on my fishing. There was not much I could do about it anyway, but as soon as I relaxed, one bat followed my fly all the way in. Astonished, I watched him catch and eat my fly, as if I were witnessing a great play at some professional sporting event.

"Oh, sh--!" I yelled to no one in particular. I looked around in embarrassment, but my son and Alan were seemingly too far away to hear me. A variety of thoughts skittered through my brain, "Was this bat dumb or nearsighted? Maybe his radar is on the fritz." But the most pressing question was, "What do I do now?"

On impact, the bat had bent my rod like a fish strike, and I heard the drag clicking. I held on to my rod and instinctively pulled back on it, inadvertently setting the hook. I was shocked when I noticed that the bat was firmly hooked and could not get off, no matter what aerial gymnastics it tried.

My son was fishing downstream, several dozen yards away, and had watched the whole episode. He had heard me shout, and realized that

I had caught something because my rod was bent and gyrating wildly, all of its own volition. But it was getting darker by the moment and he could not exactly make out what was going on. When he saw something in the air over the water, he had initially thought I had caught a fish that jumped. When my rod began to behave very differently than if I had caught a trout, he was confused.

I steadied my fly rod nearly straight up and the bat flew up, down, and around in circles, pulling against the line and the pressure of the spring in the rod. I let the bat tire himself out, as if I had been playing a trout, and slowly reeled the line in. Finally, the bat hung limp at the end of my line. I waded to shore. By this time, it was pitch dark. I hollered to my son and Alan.

"Come here and look at what I caught," I shouted. I pulled my flashlight out of my fishing vest and shined it on the bat. Both Alan and my son drew close and bent towards the light.

"What is that?" they both exclaimed.

"It's a live bat," I replied matter-of-factly, though holding the line as far as I could from my body. I explained the details of what had happened.

"It must have been a dumb bat," I concluded, "since the others were smart enough to not eat the fly."

"How are you going to unhook it?" my son asked without offering any suggestions. He has several degrees in mechanical engineering, so I thought he would have had at least one or two ideas.

"I don't know," I responded, my voice calm, despite the mild panic inside. The bat had begun to show signs of recovering from his ordeal.

I had never really thought about how to unhook a bat. Now, I still had not recovered from the shock of catching one. I once read somewhere that one in every 200 bats is rabid. I did not know if this was true or not, but even these odds did not seem to be in my favor.

"Don't bats have fangs or teeth?" I asked, trying to evaluate the problem.

"Not sure," said my son.

"Don't ask me," said Alan. "They don't teach that stuff in divinity school," he added with a laugh.

As we closely watched the bat's increasing energetic movements, we decided that it was better to just cut the line somewhere in middle of the tippet and not put my fingers close to the mouth of a bat. I did not really need to salvage the fly. I could always tie more, and besides it had already been chewed up from the previous fish.

I applied my clippers to the line while jumping backward. The bat recognized he was free and fluttered to the ground. Since the bat was still alive when I cut it off, I assumed that it would regain its strength and eventually fly off. Maybe next time this bat would be a little choosier in his evening meal selection. On the other hand, perhaps I will be more careful when casting at dusk near feeding bats.

With the descending darkness, it was clearly time to leave the stream. We followed the beams of our flashlights up the steep bank, single file, and in silence to get to our car. It had been a long day of fishing, and we were tired but content. Each of us had caught quite a few trout. Slowly, we took off our vests and waders and started putting our gear away in the trunk of the car.

"Wow, Dad!" My son exclaimed, breaking the silence. "Does your fishing license cover bats? Is taking a bat with a fishing rod legal in this state? Are bats in season? I hope they are not an endangered species! Boy, would you be in big trouble!"

Joining in the spirit of the occasion, Alan asked, "Did you remember to measure and weigh him? Maybe it was a state species record!"

I strongly suspected they were grinning, even though it was too dark to see the expressions on their faces. But it was not too dark for me to see where this was conversation was headed. When we got home, no one was going to talk about the beauty of the mountains and streams we saw, the fish we caught, the familiar camaraderie, or the good times we had. No... the only thing that was going to make the highlight reel of this fishing trip was the bat.

Georgian River, Ontario, Canada

In August of 2002, my son came home from graduate school for a few days and wanted to fish with me. Because it was August, and hot, I anticipated that fly fishing for trout would be really poor near our house this far into summer. I decided that we needed to go farther north to have any chance at catching a trout. After scouting several locations in Michigan and Canada, I decided that the farthest we could go would be to the Georgian River in Ontario. The Georgian River flows into Lake Huron.

It was more than a 500-mile trip one way. We drove to Buffalo, New York, and crossed into Canada by driving over the Peace Bridge. We both had our passports and waved them at the guard, but he only asked us where we were going and why. We told him we were going fly fishing in the Georgian River in Ontario. He did not even look inside our passports, and this was after the attack on September 11, 2001. We knew that there is a duty-free store on the Canadian side of the border and customs station and promised ourselves that we would stop at the store on the way back. We also noted the names of wineries in the area, mostly selling ice wines. We took the Queen Elizabeth Highway to Hamilton and drove through Guelph on our way north. Our first stop was at Georgian River Outfitters to pick up our Canadian fishing licenses and talk to the proprietor, John. Following John's advice, we used olive caddis larvae, adult caddis, adult mayflies (dry), and bead head mayfly nymphs.

We fished during the day at the Trestle Pool with no luck. While we were fishing there, we met Bob Tupper, a retired power company engineer and fisherman, who lives nearby and loves to fly fish. He even had a 'fishing' business card. He guided us to the Tombstone hole and told us what to use. We had no luck there, but Bob was a very colorful character and acted as a pretty good guide. I offered him some money for his services as a guide, but he refused.

We had dinner nearby and that evening we fished the outflow of Georgian River Lake Dam. The dam was very deep and its discharge kept the water temperature in the stream at the base of the dam cool, even in August. It was a steep hike from the parking lot near the dam to the river gorge below. While we were fishing we saw a large blue heron, standing perfectly still on the other side of the stream not too far from us. They are supposed to be great anglers, but he did not catch any fish either.

That night we stayed at the Three Seasons Bed & Breakfast, just south of the river, and almost across the street from the Georgian Gorge Provincial Park. The B&B was simply some spare bedrooms in the owner's house. Claudia and her husband were our gracious hosts. I forgot to pack my pajamas and he let me use an old pair of his.

They served us sherry and some small cookies in the evening. We spent more than two hours discussing politics, the economy, popular entertainment, and local news.   They said that the person who most influenced their lives was Alan Greenspan, then Chairman of the Federal Reserve (U.S.), because Canadian banks followed in lock step the interest rate movements of the Fed. They resented this state of affairs. It was a great discussion and fun to get a Canadian's viewpoint of U.S. affairs.

The next morning, Claudia made us a wonderful breakfast and we went to fish under the hydroelectric power lines.   We saw many fish jumping in the morning. I missed a big fish that hit my fly on the second cast, and had five other hits of smaller fish, landing three of them. Naturally, the one that got away was bigger than any I actually caught!

On the way home, we remembered to stop for a while at the duty-free store and purchased some liquid refreshment.

After returning home, I sent Bob some tippet material, a selection of flies I had tied, and a nice letter to say thanks for helping us on the stream. I cannot help but like Canadians. Most of them are really nice people.

Fishing for One Day in Alaska

What kind of fly fisherman would travel to Alaska and then only fish for one day? As unlikely as this may seem, that is exactly what happened. Whenever I would go to professional conferences or tradeshows, I would always ask my wife if she wanted to come along. Asking her to come along was routine. She always said, "No". This was routine, too. But when I asked her if she wanted to go to a conference in Alaska, she said, "Yes." I was caught off guard, but felt I had to honor the request. So in September of 2000, my wife and I went to Anchorage, Alaska, for a technical conference. As usual, the conference started on a Monday. We took this opportunity to arrive in Anchorage on the Friday before the conference. We were amazed that the flight from Seattle to Anchorage was almost as long as our flight to Seattle.

We stayed in at a bed and breakfast in Anchorage Friday night, and planned to drive to Seward on Saturday, stay in Seward Saturday night, and drive back to Anchorage on Sunday. Between Anchorage and Seward lies the Kenai Peninsula, one of the most well-known salmon fisheries in North America. It features the Kenai River, the Russian River and the Copper River. I knew that if I went to Alaska, I had to fish this area.

On most airline flights, the airline attendant tries to take the angler's fly rod and case from him or her, and the flight to Seattle was no exception. The angler has to fight the attendant to keep it, explaining that the rod costs more than the airfare. On the ride to Anchorage on Alaska Airline, it seemed that about half the people on the flight had fly rod cases and the attendant was very helpful, giving me the option to stow it in the Captain's closet or in the overhead bin. In this case, she emphasized that these were all very safe places. She said not to put it on the floor as it may be stepped on. I appreciated this kind of service. I immediately decided that they were going to get my future business.

After talking with someone from a fishing store where I purchased my Alaska fishing license I decided to fish at the Russian River campground where the Russian River empties into the Kenai River. I was told that there was good public access and the water was "wade-able."

I had made some 'flesh pattern' flies specifically for this trip. Flesh patterns are meant to resemble the flesh of dead salmon, which the live salmon eat.

My wife and I drove Saturday morning south to Seward. The distance was 128 miles but after we left the vicinity of Anchorage, there were only three restaurants alongside this entire highway. We stopped at one alongside the Kenai River but it was closed due to a wedding reception. We had to drive to the next one many miles away that was fortunately also alongside the river. There were many fishermen standing on our side of the river and drift boats were coming down the river.

The Kenai River was a beautiful turquoise blue-green color. We learned that this color indicated that the water came from the melt of a glacier. The restaurant was called Gwin's, at milepost 52 on the Sterling Highway at Cooper's Landing, and in my experience, the restaurant was unique. It was on the opposite side of the road from the river and the only sign of civilization. The floor was made from logs sawn in half. The floor was also covered in river water. Almost all of the patrons of the restaurant were wearing waders with the top turned down. All the anglers stopped fishing for a while, ate in the restaurant, and then resumed fishing. They did this all without removing their waders. My wife and I were the only patrons dressed normally. I guess that if you look at from the fisherman's point of view, we were the abnormally dressed ones! The food was good and not all that expensive. Gwin's has an attached general store, where I bought a shirt. A series of lodges (cabins) for fishermen surround the parking lot of the store.

When we finally entered the Russian River campground, large signs said, "Beware of the bears." It contained a list of about ten "do's" and "don'ts." My wife was quite afraid of running into a bear.

As I was putting on my waders and stringing up my rod, a forest ranger in a pickup truck parked next to us. A large dog accompanied him. I asked the ranger if the dog was government issue and he laughed and said, "Yes." I asked him if the dog could find a bear. He said, "Yes, but only a dead one." Now it was my turn to laugh.

My wife and I walked down the trail to the stream with the ranger and the dog. Steps had been cut into the side of the hill and a wooden boardwalk paralleled the stream for a while which was nice. We stopped to fish and the ranger kept going. My wife stayed on the lookout for bears while I fished. My wife saw a salmon jump right at my feet, but I didn't see it. I was casting to the far side of the stream at the time. The stream was littered with many carcasses of dead salmon but there did not appear to be a run in progress. I fished for a while and caught one silver salmon. There were a few other fisherman on the stream and they said fishing was slow, as it was getting near the end of the season.

We drove to Seward where we spent the night. As we were driving back to Anchorage the next day, we saw several streams no more than five feet wide with hundreds of large spawning salmon in them. Sometimes we saw many people standing on both banks of these streams watching the action. I had never seen such a large concentration of fish in my life!

Sadly, the remainder of the trip was taken up with business, and I could not get away to do any more fishing. As our plane took off to fly to Seattle, I looked down on all the streams and lakes dotting the landscape. I vowed to come back again when I could to do more fishing.

The Six Curious Girls

On the Saturday after September 11, 2001, a day that profoundly changed America, my daughter and I did something very ordinary. We went fly fishing in Pennsylvania in the mountains near the center of the state. We had booked a Bed and Breakfast near Rybersburg far ahead of time and felt that we might lose our deposit if we cancelled at the last minute. After weighing the pros and cons and doing some soul searching, we decided to go fishing anyway. If we cancelled, we felt that this would indicate fear on our part, and the terrorists would have won some small, indefinable victory.

During the 350-mile, six-hour drive from our house to Rybersburg, the weather was sunny and the sky deep blue with only a few white clouds. We knew of the ban on air travel, and kept looking at the sky. As expected, there were no contrails visible, but this still looked very strange. We saw six identical golden Labrador retriever puppies at an interstate rest stop that had been in a bathroom tissue television commercial. The owners of these puppies let them out to play (and pee, I'm sure). This attracted the attention of young and old alike, and was a welcome sign of normalcy.

We arrived at the B&B late in the day. It was located on a one and a half lane local country road. The B&B was a restored stone farmhouse, built in the middle of the 19th century. The house was only fifteen feet from the road, and surrounded by large old oak trees, which shaded the house. There was no front yard, just a myriad of colorful flowers filling the area between the house and the edge of the road. A faded sign indicated that parking was just off the street near the side of the house. The pasture fence of a Mennonite dairy farm stood on the other side of the road not more than twenty feet from the parking area.

Upon arrival, we went into the house to register. We introduced ourselves to the proprietress, Maria, who was about 65 years old and wore a kitchen apron over a faded dress. She had gray hair, a delightful accent, and told us she ran the B&B by herself.

"Where are you from?" I asked, my curiosity getting the best of me.

"I'm from Germany," she said. "I emigrated here many years ago." It was wonderful speaking with her, not only because of her accent, but because she had a very sunny outlook on life. We had booked a two-room suite rather than two separate rooms to save money, but Maria said that no one else was staying there that weekend, so each of us could have separate suites. I was sure that the B&B was not normally this empty, and wondered to myself how many cancellations she received.

Down the hill, not more than thirty yards behind the house, was Buck Creek. This is a famous trout stream, and the main reason we booked this B&B. I decided to go out and look at the stream conditions. To my surprise dirty yellow foam was floating on the surface of the stream, carried downstream by the current.

After reconnoitering the stream, I walked up the hill and back to the house.

"Are those soap suds?" I asked Maria, nodding toward the stream.

"Yes," she said.

"When did this happen?" I asked.

"It has been coming on for a long time," she responded. "It is unfortunate, but the increasing population pressure and poor septic systems are contributing to the decreased quality of the creek water. It is particularly bad today."

I decided that we were not going to fish Buck Creek on this trip. We needed some other spot, and Little Fishing Creek came to mind.

"How far is Little Fishing Creek?" I asked Maria.

"Not far," she responded, "only about five miles away." I hoped Little Fishing Creek was fishable. I knew that it had a good reputation, too, but I had not researched it before the trip.

"Oh well," I said. "The patterns that I had tied for Buck Creek should work on Little Fishing Creek. Same insects," I reasoned. "It's not that far away, just on the other side of the nearby mountain."

After registering, we went back out to the car to retrieve our clothes and toiletries. Immediately six cows that were grazing in the field across the street gathered at the barbed wire fence and looked over it at my daughter and me. All six stared right at us without a sound, and watched us unload very intently. It was slightly unnerving because they were only a few feet away. I ignored them, thinking that this was a coincidence. They must have been nearby in the field when we went in to register and I had not noticed them.

Our rooms were on the second floor. They were beautiful and full of antiques. The floors were wooden and highly polished. The walls were covered in antique wallpaper and decorated with black and white photographs of scenes and people from the 19th century, and every room had a fireplace. It felt like I was stepping back in time.

Before turning in, I went down to the first floor of the B&B to discuss breakfast times with Maria. I found her in her kitchen, working in the midst of glass-fronted cupboards filled with canning jars full of colorful fruits and vegetables. An iron rack full of copper pots hung over the island where she stood. I noticed that the stove looked new, and the style was like something found in a restaurant. I hoped this meant she was a good cook.

"Maria," I asked, "Can we have an early breakfast?"

"Early breakfasts are my specialty," she said. "After all, I cater to fly fishermen just like you."

Before dawn the next morning, my daughter and I went down to the kitchen. Maria made us a five-course breakfast. As we tucked in, we discovered to our delight, that she was a really good cook. Just as it was getting light enough to see, we loaded our car for the day, and sure enough, all six cows came over and watched us, almost as if they were waiting for us.

We fished that day near Taylorsville on Little Fishing Creek below the hatchery. The water was crystal clear, and we saw many fish swimming in the stream. The trout appeared to be taking something off the surface but we could not determine what it was. They ignored our dry flies. We then switched to nymphs, thinking that the trout were taking something just under the surface. After we changed nymph patterns, the trout followed, but only for the first few times we presented them. In the end, the trout would not take our nymphs either. My daughter and I tried every fly in my box but we were thoroughly skunked. Not even a nibble. That evening we went back to the B&B and the cows gathered again and intently watched us unload our gear.

"Maria," we finally asked, "do these cows always behave this oddly?"

"Oh, the girls," Maria laughed. "Yes, they know everyone's business."

The next morning we had another wonderful breakfast, paid our bill and thanked Maria profusely for her hospitality.

"Thank you so much," we said, "For the breakfasts and the lodging."

"You are welcome," she said. "Please come again. I am sorry that you did not catch any trout."

We were the only guests the entire weekend. As we packed the car, the six girls came over and watched us again. This time we expected them and laughed.

"Goodbye, girls," we shouted and waved from the car as they watched us drive away.

"Auf wiedersehen" I added with a laugh, thinking that maybe the cows understood Pennsylvania Dutch!

On the way back home, we stopped at the local fly shop near the largest town in the area and told them our tale of woe.

"Shouldn't the same flies work?" I asked. "The two streams are only five miles apart." What did we do wrong?"

"That stretch of Little Fishing Creek has thousands of trout per mile. It sees tremendous fishing pressure, and the trout are very selective," said the owner.

"You simply didn't have the right fly. You should have used a #26 cream midge," he added. So before we left the store, I bought a few to use as a tying pattern.

Although we did not catch anything this trip, we felt slightly patriotic, and that somehow we had struck a blow for democracy.

Over the winter, I tied several dozen of these flies. The next summer found us back in this area for a long weekend, staying at a B&B in Belmonte this time. We fished all the local creeks, and armed with this fly, Little Fishing Creek to great success. This entire episode reinforced the lesson of calling ahead to local fly shops to obtain stream conditions and other useful information prior to the actual outing. It was doubly satisfying that we had finally conquered Little Fishing Creek, too.

How I Acquired My First Bamboo Fly Rod

In the spring of 2002, a piece of equipment at my company needed to be repaired. The repair person flew in from Wisconsin the night before. He started working on our instrument early in the morning and really wanted to finish our job to catch a plane home in the late afternoon.

Before noon, he realized that he was running a little behind schedule, so I had a pizza delivered to our office for lunch. This was to save him time so he could finish our repair and still catch his flight. I decided to accompany him for lunch. We talked about many things but eventually he mentioned that he saw my fly fishing stuff on the walls in my office and wanted to know if I was a fly fisherman.

"Yes," I said. "I am." He then told me that his father was a fly fisherman, too, but had passed away many years ago. Furthermore, he said that his dad had owned a bamboo fly rod, which was still in his attic. He said that his dad purchased it used in 1971. He said that the wood was split, the metal was all tarnished, and the threads frayed and dull. In addition, the varnish had been rubbed off over the years leaving the wood bare. The bag it came in suffered from dry rot.

"I would be happy to purchase it from you, sight unseen," I said. He said that he did not want to rob me so we agreed on a price of $20. He said how about shipping? I said that I would throw in $6 for UPS. So we shook hands on a deal and I gave him $26 in cash. He promised to ship it in a pipe so that UPS would not break it further. I then promptly forgot about it.

About two weeks later, a metal pipe showed up at my office, delivered by UPS. I immediately realized what it was and eagerly opened the package. He was right; the rod looked like it would never work again. It was a three-piece rod about nine feet long and had two tips. He was also right in that I probably paid too much just to look at it. But since I owned it, I felt I might as well get a professional opinion. I called the local fishing store, appropriately called "The Rod Shop" and asked them where they have bamboo repaired.

Now The Rod Shop is locally owned, and a good fishing store, with a fly fishing section larger than most. But I knew that they personally didn't repair bamboo fly rods. They gave me the name and phone number of John Waggoner of Waggoner Rods located in Paris Heights. They said that this person makes new split cane bamboo rods, so he probably could repair an old one. Waggoner was located only a few miles from my office. John said that he would be willing to look at it. When could I bring it over? We arranged for me to take the rod over at lunchtime one day the following week.

I took the rod over to him and saw that he had a bamboo rod manufacturing shop in his garage. He showed me how he made rods and what the steps were. He showed me the books he used as bibles to his craft, the custom equipment he made for rod building. He showed me some rods he had made that he was selling for $4,500. He looked at my rod and said that he would do the repair and restoration for $200 but could guarantee nothing. It may never fish again and maybe the only thing I could do with the rod when he was done was to hang it over my mantel. I said, "OK, try anyway." He said that he would call me in 3-4 months when it was done. About six weeks later, he called me. He said that he had completed restoring the rod and I could come over and pick it up. This was a few days before Father's Day and I thought that this would make a nice father's day present for me. My wife went with me to pick up the rod.

We arrived and he showed me the rod. It looked fantastic. He was very proud of the restoration job he had done. The metal gleamed, the cork looked like new, all the threads were bright colors matching what I imagined the original looked like, and the varnish sparkled. He closed the split in the bamboo.

"Instead of you paying me $200," John asked, "Would you accept $400 for the rod?"

"If he would give me that much for the rod, how much could he sell it for?" I immediately thought.

"No, thanks," I responded after a moment of hesitation. He just laughed.

"Well, in that case," he said, "The rod is a Heddon Thorobred No. 14, and from the markings, it was made between 1933 and 1939. It is approximately a six-weight rod, but this weight designation did not come about until much later."

"You will have to choose between hanging this on the mantel as a showpiece or using it on the stream," he said

"The bamboo had seasoned for 70 years and that this will enable the rod to work better than when it was new," he added. "The seasoned wood will be very responsive. It will load and unload with a lot of power when you cast." He then made an allusion that the rod would move "lively" like a Stradivarius violin "resonates" where the wood (in both cases) has been aging for many years.

I have been using the rod ever since. The sensitivity of the rod is such that I can feel the action of the fly at the end of a 75-foot line. It works better that any of my fancy high bulk modulus graphite rods. I can cast farther and more accurately than with any of my other rods.

I try not to take it on an airplane, but if I do, I use a 'bomb proof' rod case that I purchased for just such an eventuality. I have absolutely no idea how much the rod is actually worth, but if I ever break it, I know just where to take it to have it repaired. John does good work!

Bar Harbor, Maine

In August of 2003, my wife and I went on vacation to New England. During our trip, we picked up our daughter, who was living at the time in Salem, Massachusetts, and drove on to Bar Harbor, Maine, for the weekend. While there, my daughter and I wanted to fly fish. I called ahead and located a guide, Bill Sprout. Bill agreed to guide us for ½ day for $150. We told him that we only had freshwater gear and could not fly fish in salt water.

"OK," he said. "I will arrange something. You need to bring sink tip lines for what I have in mind."
"We can do that," I replied. "See you there!"

The guide picked us up at the prearranged time at our hotel in Bar Harbor in his pickup truck on a Sunday morning. He drove us to a small lake behind a blueberry packing plant. The pond was the source of fresh water for the packing plant. Apparently, these plants use lots of water.

On the way to the pond, he told us about some famous clients of his. For example, he guided a famous actor from Hollywood last year, and had just guided two football players from the Cincinnati Bengals. He was about to continue along this same vein when my daughter said, "Well, we bring your average down, because we are nobody." He laughed and shut up.

The guide took many short cuts on small roads to get to the pond. I was becoming certain that he was trying to confuse us, as to the location of the pond to keep it a secret. Then when we got to the blueberry plant, we turned down a single lane dirt road with very deep ruts. When we arrived at the pond, he parked the truck, took out some float tubes and told us how to get in and out of them. This was quite a trick since the wearer had to put oversized fins on his or her fishing boots, but we quickly mastered it. Both my daughter and I were nervous about getting into these, but they turned out to be very stable and worked just fine. He told us to keep alert for any motion along the shoreline, because bears had been recently spotted near the pond.

I measured the water temperature of the surface of the pond. It was 74°F. The guide told us the temperature 20 feet down was 54°F, just right for trout. I caught a 17-inch brook trout on a # 14 prince nymph with a sink tip line. The guide caught a few smaller trout. The guide helped direct my daughter to various "good" spots since he knew where the fish hid, but she did not catch anything that morning. We tried fishing at spots all over the pond following his directions. In order to navigate the float tube, the wearer has to kick his or her feet. There was a slight breeze, which continued to blow us in one direction to the far end of the pond. We always had to move our feet just to stay in one spot if the wind was blowing.

We took many pictures with our digital camera and my daughter later used these to impress her co-workers at the company she was working at, so it was not a total loss for her. We both had a good time.

The guide did not know it, but I had my handheld GPS tracking device with me. As we were leaving, I turned it on and pushed the 'position capture' button. Using my GPS "topographical" and street map software, I later found out that the place we went was named Simmonds Pond, which is located in Ellicott, Maine, very close to Bar Harbor, so much for his misdirection and secret place!

One Memorial Day Weekend

My daughter and I went fishing on Saturday of Memorial Day Weekend. We went to Oak Creek, but first we had to stop for breakfast at The Arcadian in Tinkersville. We arrived slightly before 8:00 AM, and it was a good thing we arrived early, because slightly after that, the place filled up with local customers. We both ordered the pancakes and they were spectacularly good.

When we arrived at Oak Creek, we observed that the water was high and muddy. We could not wade across the creek to fish at the place where we caught many fish the previous year. Because of the water level, we were restricted to the road side of the stream. My daughter caught a 10-inch trout on her first cast on a #14 Sulfur nymph. The trout was shiny and silver all over. She claimed that the fish jumped out of the water to eat the nymph as it was approaching the water on her cast.

I did not see it so I did not know. I can speculate, without much incredulity, that a trout might be tempted to hit on a dry fly in the air but not a nymph. My daughter is usually truthful, and I have seen even stranger things happen. Maybe the best explanation is that the trout got confused. We'll never know. I missed a fish on my third cast with the same fly as soon as it touched the surface of the stream, but caught one a few casts later.

Shortly after this incident, an old fly fisherman stopped to talk to us on the stream. I told him that my daughter and I had each caught one fish on a #14 sulfur nymph, but that was all. He told me that he and his fishing buddy had not caught anything yet that morning. He admired my bamboo fly rod and asked where I got it. I told him the story about buying it sight unseen, and having it restored. He told me he had been looking for bamboo fly rods at flea markets for several years, but had not seen one that he felt was worth the price.

I asked him if he had ever cast a bamboo fly rod before.

"No, I haven't," he replied.

"Would you like to?" I asked, handing him my rod. I explained that the rod action would be much slower than he was use to as he fished with a graphite rod. I invited him to cover my patch of water with the bamboo rod. He did so, without getting any hits, but thanked me very much for the opportunity.

We told each other that we tied our own flies. He looked at our fly selection and we looked at his. He gave us a bead head nymph pattern with sparkling olive dubbing which he had personally designed and tied. He claimed worked well on Oak Creek.

"I have been coming here for more than 20 years and consider this creek my home waters. This fly with catch fish when nothing else will. Put it on your tippet and try it," he urged.

Upon reflection, a lot of good this fly did him, as he had not caught anything yet. I gave him several of the Blue Wing Olives I had tied as a suitable exchange. This seemed to be good fishing etiquette.

"I mostly don't tie wings, only parachute-style dry flies," he said as he examined the flies I gave him.

Thinking that there may be something in his claim about the nymph's ability to attract fish in this stream, I chose not use it that day, on the chance that I might lose it. I decided that I would take it home and reverse engineer it first.

We had no other strikes nor did we see any other fish. The water was too high, muddy and fast. We tried other nymph patterns and some Light Cahill and Sulfur dry flies and some Blue Wing Olives, too, but no luck. The steam conditions were not good.

We then drove to Taneda and ate at the Soda Cup Restaurant next to the County Sport Shop, a fly fishing store. Taneda is a small town. Later I learned that Taneda has a population of 600 and the entire county has a population of less than 5,000. A paraphrased sign in the Soda Cup Restaurant in Taneda read, "A man is on a stream, fly fishing, and there is no woman around to hear him. He speaks. Is he still wrong?" It was that kind of place. My daughter and I looked at each other, knowing that this was misogynistic, but said nothing. My daughter was a better fly fisher 'person' than most men, and I was proud of her. She had great eye-hand coordination and could cast a fly a long distance with light tackle under just about any weather and stream conditions.

We talked to Don, the proprietor of the fishing store. We showed him the sparkling bead head nymph pattern and he sold us some dubbing that was close in color, texture and sparkle. But it was not an exact match. I decided to try to use the material he sold me anyway to make some flies. We told Don that we were going to East Sycamore Creek. He said that the trout would hit on Light Cahills and Sulfur flies, both dry and nymph.

We drove to East Sycamore Creek after lunch to fish and noticed that there were people camping all along the creek. Each car had a semi-official paper form stuck to the back window with the blanks filled in with ink. It then dawned on me that this part of the stream was in Alleghoma National Forest and that these people had permits to camp at each location. The water was clear and not too high. We were able to cross the stream at will. Families were running and hiking up and down the length of the stream. I am sure that this scared the fish. We saw no fish at all and did not catch anything.

After returning home, I tried to recreate the fly that the old fisherman gave me. It turned out to be surprisingly difficult. The secret was in the dubbing. Altogether, I bought four different kinds of "ice" and "sparkle" dubbing from several different fly shops and manufacturers without exactly matching the sample, until I realized that the fly pattern was really a mixture of two different dubbings with a few strands of another lighter dubbing on the wings. I thought that this was somewhat clever.

With this realization, it turned out to be simple to find the different kinds of dubbing. The exact color and texture matches were Caddis Green and Sparkle Olive (1 to 1 ratio). The wings were a few strands of light olive dubbing. With that insight, I tied a dozen prototype flies and made what I think are improvements to the sample I was given. Since it is a unique pattern, I have named it the "Oak Creek Sparkle Nymph." I recorded the tying steps, will use this recipe to tie some "production" quantity nymphs, and try them on Oak Creek the next chance I get.

A year and a half later, I read in a fly-fishing magazine article that said some trout have been known to leap out of the water to eat flies. This is done primarily to chase caddis flies, which swim from the bottom to the surface of the water at a very high velocity. They continue with their upward momentum at the surface leaving the water at a very high speed, too. Mayflies on the other hand, drift up to the surface more slowly. Furthermore, the article said that trout go nuts trying to catch caddis, including leaping into the air. I now believed my daughter without any reservation, and told her about the article the next time I talked to her. She just laughed.

"Dad, I know what I saw that day," she said.

Fishing Dreams

For more than a year, Rodger and I had been planning a special fishing trip to a secluded stretch of a trout river in a state forest area north of here. This was a more than an eight-hour trip by car, a really far off destination for us. We normally considered a two- to three-hour drive a far distance for us to fish. We are fortunate in that there are many fishing opportunities within a short drive of where we live. So there was no real need for us to go any farther.

However, this trip was different. Our goal was to experience trout fishing on legendary waters, which had been written about by famous authors, such as Ernest Hemmingway. We studied maps and planned to take a canoe to reach sections of streams that are not accessible by any other means. We were hoping that this would mean a very low fishing pressure, and many hungry fish. We were planning to be away for four days, and made reservations at motels for three nights at various locations in the area and along our route.

Finally, as the day of our departure was drawing near, everything was in readiness. Then I got a call from Rodger.

"Bill," he said. "My wife has developed a hip problem. She won't be able to manage by herself while we're gone. Her sister can't come, so I have to stay home and help her. I am sorry, but I can't go." I was stunned. We had been planning this trip for a long time.

"Rodger, is your wife going to be OK?" I asked.

"Yes, but she'll need my help."

"When do you think we can reschedule the trip?" I asked.

"I don't know," he responded. "She is in a lot of pain, and may have to have surgery or go to rehabilitation. Everything is up in the air right now. Why don't you go for the both of us?" I had not considered this. I knew that it was now or never, at least for this year, as I was going to be busy at work for the remainder of the summer and would not be able to get away.

"Look," Rodger said. "Consider this a scouting trip for an even better trip next year."

"Maybe I will," I said. "I need to think this over. I'll call you back." My choice was to go now, delay for an additional year, or follow Rodger's advice and go both years. I talked this over with my wife.

"Go," she said. "You know that I don't like you going alone, in case something would happen. But I have already made plans to visit our daughter while you were going to be gone. I'm going to help her with our grandchildren and I don't want to cancel," she added.

I called Rodger back. "Rodger, I am going to go," I said.

"Good!" was his reply. "Take good notes about stream conditions, insects, and trout abundance. You know the drill, and make sure you record the GPS locations of the best spots. We will mark these places on a topo map and this will make next year's trip even better."

"It won't be as much fun without you, buddy," I said.

"Yeah, yeah, yeah," he laughed good-naturedly, a little embarrassed, but not willing to admit it. "You will be catching all the fish. That should be enough fun."

I loaded the car Wednesday evening, and very early Thursday morning kissed my wife goodbye and started driving north. She made sandwiches for me and packed a lunch. She also loaded a cooler with bottled water and a variety of soft drinks for me to consume along the way. I noticed that she put in a number of cans of caffeinated soda to keep me awake. The drive was long and sometimes boring without anyone to talk to. I listened to the radio when I was within range of a station I liked, and to a number of CDs we keep in the center console when the radio was uninteresting. I drove straight through with only bathroom and gas breaks. To amuse myself, I kept track of gas prices at stations along the route so when I drove back, I would know where the cheapest gas prices were.

I arrived at the interstate exit about 4:00 PM and turned onto a two-lane state highway. I had made good time. After 100 yards, I stopped at a local outfitter where I had arranged to pick up a Kevlar canoe I had rented for several days. The building's outside looked dilapidated. It was once painted white but this paint had mostly peeled, leaving the wood planks underneath exposed. It had a covered porch that ran the entire length of the front of building. There were wooden Adirondack chairs on the porch and a dozen canoes on racks along the side of the building in chains. There were no other cars in the parking lot.

When I pulled up, a young guy came out of the front door, walked to the front of the porch and said, "You must be the one here for the canoe."

"Yes, I am," I said.

"We were going to close, but the owner said you might be here and I should wait."

"I am glad you did. I want to get an early start tomorrow morning."

"It wouldn't have mattered much," he said. "The fish don't start biting until about 9:30 AM when the sun heats the water up a bit. We are here by 7:00 AM."

"Just the same, let's do this," I said. He selected a canoe, helped me put it on the rack on the top of my car, and showed me how to tie it down. We went into the store to sign the papers.

"Any fishing supplies, you need?" he asked, doing his salesman duty. I looked around. The place was full of fishing lures, spools of monofilament fishing line, leaders, swivels, sinkers, rods, nets, boating paraphernalia, insect repellant, boots, hats, and anything else a city slicker might have forgotten to bring with him. There was a cooler full of minnows and a refrigerator full of mealworms, red worms and nightcrawlers. The place definitely catered to the spin cast crowd.

"I'm good," I said.

I spotted an old, faded, state forest map hanging on the wall. We had planned out our trip, but I thought that this might be a good opportunity to get some advice. I pointed to a section of the map and asked, "How would I do if I fished this stretch here?"

"I've never fished there, but you would probably do well. That's a difficult place to get to, so the fish don't see many fishermen. There used to be a fishing camp there in the old days that you could only get to by boat. The state put in some roads in the '50s and '60s that made other parts of the forest more accessible so no one goes there anymore. You'd pretty much have that stretch to yourself."

I left the store, got in the car, drove almost directly across the street and into the parking lot of the Pines Motel. It was a one-story brick building with a dozen units in a "U" shape around a gravel parking lot. Tall pines surrounded the back of the motel. There was a comic aspect in all of this as tall pines also surrounded the Birchwood Motel a few yards down the street. I checked in. The room had a small refrigerator, hot plate and coffee maker in it. It was clean but sparse. I laughed out loud. There was a picture over the bed of a fisherman sitting in a Birchwood canoe netting a fish on a small stream. I thought that it was ironic that the Pines Motel would have a picture of a Birchwood canoe. There was no cell phone reception.

The next morning I got up before dawn, made myself breakfast and drank some coffee. I felt surprisingly well considering I spent most of the previous day sitting. I was also slightly excited in anticipation of what the day would hold. I left my room and took a deep breath of fresh air. The air smelled damp, clean, and of pine.

I drove about 30 minutes down the state highway, and then turned north for another 45 minutes on a gravel road, to arrive at my closest put-in. I untied the canoe, put it on the shore, and loaded all my equipment. I made sure that I had my GPS with extra batteries with me. I pushed off, deciding to paddle upstream for the first part of the day, and make notes on likely fishing spots for the return trip. Then I would fish while the current carried me downstream and back to the car. After a few strokes of the paddle, I stopped, turned my head around, and fixed the put-in place in my memory so I'd recognize it again. It would not do to pass this place on the way back and get lost. In addition, I recorded the GPS coordinates as a backup to my memory.

Morning in the woods was exhilarating. The sky was bright blue with some high cirrus clouds. There was no breeze and the temperature was cool with a hint that it would warm up later. I did not paddle hard, but just enjoyed being there. I saw many deer and raccoon tracks in the mud along the stream, and noted many spots that should hold fish. As the sun cleared the tree tops the ripples on the stream flashed and sparkled, and occasionally dew drops hanging on leaf tips looked like tiny jewels among the green streamside plants. There was deep shade under the larger trees, and sometimes I saw buttercups, black-eyed susans, and some pretty blue flowers, whose name I did not know.

The land in the park was relatively flat. The stream appeared to have made its home in a very large shallow valley. The banks were a mixture of larger stones, some gravel and some sand. Some of these stones had sharp edges; some were slightly rounded by weather and geologic time, while others were completely water-smoothed. Black dirt backed up the stones on the shores, varying from a few feet to 25 feet from the water's edge, depending upon the whims of the oxbows. There was dark mud along some banks, but this was the exception rather than the rule. As far as I could tell, there did not appear to be any silt on the stream bed. I wondered about the geology of this area. I knew this land had been covered by a glacier in the last ice age, but did not know enough to make any reasonable guesses as to how his mixture of terrain came to be.

Flying insects did not appear until about 10:00 AM, and I saw some rise rings. Very exciting signs for a fly fisherman. When I judged that I was as far up the steam as I should paddle, I stopped, ate a sandwich and drank some coffee from my thermos. I stretched my legs and rested for a short while, just listening to nature. I had seen no one all morning. Since this was a Friday, I did not expect to see any weekend fishermen yet. I strung up my rod and selected a small light colored dry fly pattern.

I turned the canoe downstream and just let it drift. I cast to many likely spots and was rewarded with strikes often enough to keep me happy and interested. The trout were mostly in the 12 to 14 inch range. I retuned them all back to the stream. I pushed the position capture button on my GPS many times. I wished that Rodger was here to share in the fun. I had already decided that we should definitely come back. If a spot was an especially a good one, I would get out of the canoe to fish. I also did this to stretch my legs from time to time.

I was so enraptured by the adventure that I lost track of time. Alerted by the lengthening shadows I finally noticed that the sun was dipping toward the horizon. For some reason, it took me a lot longer to get back to my starting point than I anticipated. I looked at my GPS and pushed a button. It told me that I had another 1,500 yards, straight-line back to my starting point. Of course, the distance would be much longer than this, as the steam did not travel in a straight line. It was getting dusk, and the light was fading. I stopped fishing altogether, and picked up the pace of my paddling.

To my complete surprise, while I was paddling around a bend, I came across another fisherman. He was the first person I had seen all day. He looked to be about 60 years old, and was fishing upstream with a dry fly. I pulled over to the far shore and stopped my canoe as a courtesy, to not spook the fish he was casting to. His casts were works of art and I marveled how perfect his timing was. He was casting a bamboo rod, and wore an old hat. His presentation was so delicate that it looked like his line did not even touch the water. I was surprised to see a trout ignore his fly, even though it was a perfect cast. I waited patiently for him to notice me. He looked up and smiled.

"Must be pretty selective trout," I say, "to ignore your offering so delicately presented."
"How did you do today?" he asked in response.
"I did good today," I answer. "How about you?"
"The name's John," he says. He said that he did not catch anything today, but he had taken many trout out of here for many years. He said he had good memories of this spot, but he had not been back for a while.

"It is just nice to be here, and remember. I always took pleasure in fly fishing this stream," he added. "It was the anticipation that anything could happen, even getting skunked. You know the old adage, 'Some days even the guide couldn't catch a fish,'" he said with a laugh.

"I even enjoyed those days. Never kept a record of how many I caught. It was just being on the stream. That was the important thing, and of course next most was who I fished with."

"Well, John, good luck to you," I said. "I have got to get back to my car before it gets completely dark." He understood what I meant, paused in his fishing and I canoed past him. When I turn around again to look at him, he was almost out of sight, but even in the fading light I could tell he was still casting.

I paddled faster and faster, looking intently at the shapes of the trees and underbrush next to the stream, while the light in the sky faded. I had a miniature flashlight in my vest, but was worried that I would not be able to find the put-in place in the dark. Then I saw it. At least it looked like a familiar patch of shoreline. I looked down, and when I saw the mark left in the dirt by my canoe that morning I became certain. Fortunately, this *was* my put-in place. I had arrived just as the sky turned pitch dark.

I beached the canoe, turned on the car engine and the head lights so I could see. I unloaded the canoe, making several trips, carrying all my gear and dragging the canoe up the hill. I tied the canoe to the top of my car, and started driving to the state highway. It was nerve racking, driving on a twisty gravel road, in the woods, in the dark. The headlights seemed to bounce up and down at every bump and pot hole. I finally made it to the highway, and as I was about to turn back the way I came, I noticed some lights in the other direction. It looked like a commercial building. As I pulled into the parking lot, I saw that it was a combination general store, restaurant, and gas station. Someone was moving around inside.

I walked in the door. The person in the store was a little, wiry, gray haired woman. She was wiping table tops.

"Excuse me," I said. "Are you still open?" She turned and looks at me. I suddenly realized how I must look. I was tired, sunburned, my hair was matted from wearing my hat all day, my clothes were dirty, and I smelled like fish.

"That depends on what ya need," she replied, sizing me up with a quick glance.

"Well, for starters, I'm famished," I responded. "I've been fishing all day and have only eaten one sandwich about nine hours ago.

"Well, I guess I can turn the stove back on," she said. "There is no other place on the main highway that ya can get to before their closing time." She reaches into a bin on one side of the counter and starts to hand me a menu.

"Never mind the menu, how about a big juicy burger? Medium well."

"I kin do that," she said, turning away with a chuckle.

In a small bathroom at a back corner of the store, I wash my hands, splash water on my face, and look at myself in the mirror, as I try to smooth my hair over with my hand. I take my time and walk back into the main room to the sound of a burger beginning to sizzle. By now I am starting to feel aches in certain muscles I overused today, as I am not use to paddling that much. I grab a bag of chips, and a soda from the cooler, sit down at the counter, and look around for the first time. The place was decorated in old fishing memorabilia. On one wall was a collage of old pictures. Many pictures included a string of 12 to 20 fish on a wooden dock with someone that looked like a lot like John and another person in front of an old building.

"Who is the guy in most of these pictures?" I asked.

"An old guide and fishing camp owner," she answered.

"Is the camp still around here?" I queried.

"The camp used to be around here, but it's been closed for a long time. The owner passed away before I was born, the summer before the war I think. They say he was the best dry fly fisherman in these here parts."

While I ate my dinner, I kept looking at the pictures. They sure looked like the person I met. It must be a coincidence. It had to be someone else who looks like John, maybe a grandson or some other relative. But even the old fishing hat looked similar. Maybe it was the hat and not the face that caused the association. Because I was so hungry, I ate quickly and asked for my check.

"No charge," she said, "for the meal, but ya can leave a tip."

"That's mighty nice of you, and I will," intending to leave a tip big enough to cover the cost of the food as well. "But why? You don't know me. I am a stranger around these parts. And I caused you extra work and expense."

"Any friend of John's is a friend o' mine," she said.

"How did you know I recognized him in the pictures?" I asked in complete astonishment.

"By the expression on yer face when I said he passed away many years ago."

The Hatch

I was fishing Oak Creek near Tinkersville one Saturday morning in early June with my fishing buddy Rodger, and we did not have any strikes at all since we started fishing at about 8:30AM.

We had been there about two weeks before and had done well, so we thought that it was worth another trip. We knew that the creek held browns, brookies and an occasional rainbow trout, and from the size of them, some of them had wintered over for two years. The Fish and Boat Commission stocks 6-inch long trout. Now under normal stream and weather conditions trout grow about two inches per year. So if an angler catches a 10-inch trout, they can figure that it has been there about two years.

After fishing all morning with no strikes it looked like our luck had run out and we were going to be skunked. This was very unusual and I was mentally trying to figure out what we were doing wrong, or how the environmental conditions were different from out last visit. I kept changing my fly to see if this would make any difference. I tried fishing with dry flies on the surface and with nymphs at various depths. With no interest at all from the trout, I just couldn't make any sense of it.

At 11:00AM, there were one or two random insects in the air. At 11:01AM, there were about two dozen, and one minute later, there were about several hundred thousand. This was a wonderful surprise. Although I knew what a hatch was, I had never seen one before. It was magnificent display of nature. They were all around me and so numerous, I had to remember to keep my mouth closed, afraid that if I didn't, one would fly in.

I knew that they were mayflies because they had tails, but not what kind. A #18 Light Cahill was the closest fly I had in my box to match the hatch. Unluckily, I was fishing a nymph when this happened. But as quick as I could, I cut the nymph off the end of my tippet with my clippers, put on the Cahill, and gave some to Rodger. Later on I verified that it was indeed a Light Cahill mayfly hatch.

The trout went crazy and the surface of the stream appeared to be boiling. On nearly every cast, I either caught a trout, a trout struck at my fly and missed, or I missed setting the hook in the trout. This was one of the fiercest, fastest, and thrilling stretches of fly fishing I had ever experienced. Forty-five minutes later the hatch disappeared almost as fast as it appeared.

As the hatch disappeared, I realized that I had been full of adrenalin, which was now slowly disappearing from my body. I discovered that many of my muscles ached and mostly I was feeling exhausted.

After the hatch, we caught nothing regardless of what we used. The trout were either sated or not interested. No fish would bite anything. It was like nothing had happened that morning and there was no trout in the stream, even though we knew that this was not true. With no activity, I started thinking about the behavior of the fish. Finally, I speculated that the reason we had no luck earlier that morning, was that the trout were somehow conditioned to wait for the hatch.

As we left the stream, all I could think of was, *"What an exciting few minutes."* I was genuinely happy to have experienced a hatch. It turned out to be a great fishing day after all. I am looking forward to my next hatch and hope that it does not take too many years before I experience it. I now actively search out hatches and take advantage of them whenever my work schedule and the timing of mother nature coincide.

Sault Ste. Marie, Ontario, Canada

One summer, my wife and I decided to take a vacation to Michigan in August. Because we were intending to travel to the upper Michigan peninsula, I wanted to use this opportunity to fly fish in Canada for a few hours. Originally I wanted to drive 20 additional miles into Canada from Sault Ste. Marie to fish for trout, but the Bed & Breakfast (B&B) I wanted to stay at was full for the approaching bear hunting season.

When I called a B&B in Sault Ste. Marie to make overnight reservations the owner said, "Why don't you fish right over the hill? Many of our customers do. We are world famous for the salmon runs."

The B&B was located across the road from the St. Mary River. I decided to fish in this area and called the local fishing store. They gave me the name of the local fishing guide, Norm. I called Norm and he told me I ought to use a 3-inch Magog Smelt pattern. I looked this pattern up on the internet and synthesized the best features of two or three different designs, which I tied along with a salmon streamer for use on the river when I got there. I arranged to meet Norm at 8:00PM the evening before my fishing day.

On the way into Michigan we traveled north on Route US 23. This road goes right by a big box outdoor superstore. Naturally, we had to stop and I used part of a $100 gift certificate I was given for Father's Day to purchase a wading staff that I had been wanting. The first night of our vacation, we stopped at a town in Michigan known for Christmas items. We went into the Christmas store. It might have been a good store, but did not live up the hype and expectations generated by the numerous billboard advertisements, starting 200 miles away. However, we did find an angel to put on top of our Christmas tree.

The second night we stayed on Mackinaw Island, Michigan. The island is in Lake Huron near the strait that connects Lake Michigan to

Lake Huron and separates Michigan's Upper and Lower peninsulas about 4.5 miles from the mainland. The Mackinac Bridge enables I-75 to cross this body of water. There is no bridge to the island and anyone who wants to visit must take a passenger ferry to get there. The island does not permit personal cars, so bicycles were everywhere. We stayed at a Bed and Breakfast right next to the harbor. It was very charming.

The next day we drove north across Michigan's Upper Peninsula and crossed the border from Sault Ste. Marie, Michigan to Sault Ste. Marie, Ontario, Canada. The English translation of this name is the Saint Mary's Rapids. This is accurate since the Saint Mary's river descends about 21 feet in the space of ¼ mile. The rapids there are very nice for fishing. There are locks on the river called the Soo Locks. The Soo locks can accept ships up to 105 feet wide and 1000 feet long. They are on both the U.S. and Canadian side and permit large ocean going ships to pass. This river is about 21 miles long, connects Lake Superior to Lake Huron and is vital to shipping in the Great Lakes. There are five salmon runs per year in this river. Wading access is only possible from the Canadian side.

When we arrived in Sault Ste. Marie, Ontario, I bought a one-day Canadian fishing license for $16.50 CDN for the Great Lakes Waterways only. I met Norm at 8:00PM in the evening. He showed me how to get across the canal at the Canadian locks and where to fish under the Sault Ste. Marie International Bridge (I-75 in the US). This also included a trek across an island in the river, which has been converted into a natural park. The angler must walk the width of this island just to arrive at the river's edge. There is a low dam across the river at this point to aid in navigation.

He told me that there was no salmon run in progress at this time, and if there were any fish, I would find them in deep holes. He said that while the river was only a few feet deep in most places in the rapids, that there were 13-foot deep holes that I should fish in and to not fall in. We stood on the shore and he pointed out where I needed to fish. I paid him $25 CDN for his time. I showed him the flies I tied and asked him if they would work. He looked them over, exclaimed how nice they were, and opined that they should work just fine. The reason for the evening meeting was that he was not available to guide me the next morning.

The next morning I fished from 6:00 to 8:00AM. This necessitated that I get up before dawn and arrive at the parking lot to wait for enough light to see. One other fisherman was already in the parking lot, sitting in his car. As soon as he saw me get out of my car he literally threw his fishing gear on and ran down the path. I wished he would have waited as I would have asked his advice.

When I got to the water, a half-mile hike, he was already way out in the river ahead of me. The Canadian side has a fish ladder. I waded through the ladder, which was separated from the river rapids by a low (four-foot tall concrete wall). The depth of the water in the ladder was about two feet. There were no fish transiting the ladder. Not a good sign. I estimated that the river was about 400 yards wide at that point. The bridge was a high-level one about 2.8 miles long (with 128 feet clearance) to permit ocean going ships to pass underneath it.

I only caught one salmon, and felt lucky to do so, but had a good time anyway, wading the rapids. I was a little afraid of the holes, but moved slowly and was very careful where I waded. I used my new wading staff to test the depth before I moved a step. Now I can say that I fished for salmon in Canada.

We then drove to Traverse City, Michigan, and stayed at a B&B right on the Boardman River called Whispering Waters. The B&B was on the far side of the river. Visitors had to drive over the river on his driveway to get to there. The river was only about 15-20 yards wide but looked beautiful. I showed the owner and another guest my fly collection. The owner said there was no run right now but I was welcome to wet my line, which I did. He watched me cover a dozen yards of waterfront shoreline with no hits, and invited me to come back and fish with him in the spring on his property when the fishing is great.

On the way back home we drove along the Grayling River and though the town of Grayling, Michigan. There were several fly fishing stores in the town and "fly fishing only" areas all along the river.

When I arrived back home I tied up a few more Smelt patterns and Salmon streamer patterns to mail to Norm by way of saying thanks again for his help. He sent me an email thanking me, and suggested that I come in the fall when the Salmon run and fish from his boat at the base of the rapids. Furthermore, he said the fishing was world class during the Salmon runs. I intend to take him up on this invitation.

How I Found and Restored My Second Bamboo Rod

I had been corresponding with Chris, a manager at an environmental cleanup company in Brattleboro, Vermont. He was a customer of mine. During one of our many discussions, I found out that he was a fly fisherman too. We talked business mostly, but we also occasionally talked about fly fishing. Chris said he liked living in Brattleboro, but described it as, "Way out in the boondocks."

Chris said the Connecticut River flows through the town, and there were many streams and lakes nearby, not to mention many state parks too. He described the fly fishing in that area as great. Finally, in September of 2006, I made a sales call to his company. During my visit, Chris gave me an old split cane bamboo rod. It was not fishable in its present condition. When he gave it to me, he said that his father bought it in the late 1960s at an estate sale in Vermont.

I took the rod for evaluation to John Waggoner, a master bamboo rod maker of J. F. Waggoner Rods located in Paris Heights. He looked at the rod and pronounced its apparent doom.

"This rod is mass produced and is looked down upon by the collecting community," he said. "These ferrules were staked on with blind stakes. This is the reason the tips are shorter than the other pieces. The ferrules on those pieces are broken off. I wouldn't waste my time restoring this since it has no collectable value."

I was greatly disappointed to hear this as I was planning to give this rod as a gift to my daughter.

"What if I were to restore this rod myself?" I asked. "How much would your charge me for the parts I need?"

"I'll get a list of parts together and let you know," he responded. "This rod was made in the 1920s by Horrocks-Ibbotson, Montague or Chubb," he said. "Since this rod has two tips, it may have been a slightly more upscale rod." He went through the motions of casting the rod a few times.

"The rod action still feels pretty good," he judged. "This rod will fish as either a size five or 6-weight rod. In the 1920s these size designations had not been invented yet."

John then went on to tell me how I could determine more precisely the rod's maker and manufacturing date. Through John's direction and suggestions, I later determined that it was a Horrocks-Ibbotson fly rod made in Utica, NY in the 1920s. Although no name was visible, I could make the identification by the red agate in the stripper guide; the shape, color and features of the reel seat; the presence and location of decorative wrappings; and matching the ferrule shape and construction. This was pretty conclusive.

John called me less than a week later. He told me the cost of the repair parts would be about $100.

I told him to go ahead and order the parts. I would come in and pick them up when he called me.

He said I should start my restoration using a mild varnish stripper to remove the old varnish while I was waiting for the parts to arrive.

About a month later, John called saying that all the parts were in, and I arranged to visit him the next day. When I arrived, he had all the parts laid out and explained to me how to remove the old parts, strip the rod down to the bare wood, and replace the parts with new ones as necessary. He said that any good polyurethane varnish would do for the finish. I took notes intending to complete the job myself without any further explanations, but he laughed and said that I would be calling him several times. I told him that I own the Wayne Cattanauch, Garrison/Carmichael, and Elser/Mauer classic bamboo fly rod books that he had recommended I buy several years ago. He said that they were good, and would help me, but he still expected some calls. I thanked him profusely.

That evening I went to work to begin the restoration process. I cleared all the thread and guides off the bamboo in the manner he demonstrated to me. I removed the ferrules from the two tips, and the butt section by pulling the stakes out. I could not immediately remove the ferrules on the mid-section or the reel seat because these stakes were almost flush with the surface and I could not get a good purchase with the tools I had at home.

I brought these parts to work and discussed removal strategies with a mechanical engineer who worked for me. He is not only an engineer but also a mechanical genius, having built many assemblies of small electrical and mechanical parts for NASA (for use in space). I guess he fit the definition of a rocket scientist! He was able to pull out one pin and drill out the other two. I then applied heat. All the remaining ferrules and the reel seat came off easily.

I then removed the cork and the wooden filler under the reel seat. The bamboo was split in this section. I noticed that there was a loose piece of bamboo on the midsection too. At this point, I realized that I needed John's professional help. I called him again and made an appointment to see him over my lunch hour for a few minutes. He laughed and said he knew I would be calling.

I drove to his house on a very snowy Friday in January. He was preparing to go to a trade show in Somerset, New Jersey, called the Fly Fishing Show. He looked at the rod and said that I did a very good job of stripping it, and told me how to proceed.

To repair the rod in the mid-section where a small piece of bamboo was loose, he recommended that in addition to gluing, I wrap the rod in that area, completely covering that section of the rod with white silk thread and then paint it with Tung oil. He told me the Tung oil will cause the thread to turn transparent, and the extra wraps will add strength to this area. He gave me a partial spool of the white silk thread to use.

I asked him about the decorative wraps spaced about every 4-5 inches on the rod that I removed prior to stripping. He said that it was a matter of taste whether I wanted to put them back on. In the early days these additional wraps were to help provide strength to hold the rod together since glues were not that strong. He said that it does not matter with today's epoxies and glues.

He looked through all my parts and asked, "Where is the hook keeper." I told him I remember taking off the hook keeper and thought that I put it in the bag. I looked through the parts in the bag and could not find it. He graciously gave me another ring hook keeper to put on, just in case I could not find the one I took off. I offered to pay him for this, but he said, "No, it wasn't worth writing up the order."

I thanked him profusely for his graciousness, his time, all his advice, and for the hook keeper and wished him well at his show. I said that I hoped I would not have to bother him again. He laughed saying this should get me going for a while and to come back when I had more questions. He then emphasized that I would have more questions.

That weekend I glued the rod, both midsection and butt sections using the crisscross cotton string method John showed me and left them to dry. The next day I removed the string and the excess glue from the surface of the rod. This worked well. The rod looked fantastic, and the pieces appeared to be strongly bonded together with tight joints.

After all the ferrules were glued on the bamboo, the next step was to space the guides. There are two tip sections with this rod and one tip section is longer than the other. After some experimentation and calculation, I decided to use the spacing recommended in my bamboo rod textbooks.

I then tied on all the guides using the techniques in the textbooks. I also put on a red decorative wrap on the butt section where no guide is needed to continue the spacing and pattern of the wraps. This was not necessary, but looked aesthetically pleasing. After I finished wrapping the guides, I painted the silk with Tung oil and let it dry. Tung oil does not stand up to moisture so I had to cover it with varnish. Finally, I put three coats of Marine Spar Varnish on the rod, sanding lightly with 800 grit sand paper between coats.

I wrote on the rod that I dedicated it to my daughter. When I showed her the finished rod she read the inscription under the varnish, and was at a loss for words; probably one of the few times in her life. She just said, "Aww" and that she would keep it for the rest of her life. Then she wanted me to keep it and use it, but I said, "No, this is yours to use on a stream. I already have one." She asked, "When do we go?" I answered, "In the spring after the ice breaks!" In one of my trips to her apartment, I took the rod in the case and left it there for her to keep. She said that if there was ever a fire, the rod was one of the things she would save.

I reminded her of the time on Oak Creek when she was with me and an older fisherman marveled over my restored bamboo rod. I said, "Just think, of all of the freshwater fisherman in the United States, only 10% are fly fisherman, of those fly fisherman only 10% own and use a bamboo rod, and of the bamboo rod users, and even smaller percentage use antique restored bamboo rods. What are the chances that two anglers standing side by side on a stream are both using antique restored bamboo fly rods? Practically zero! I think it will be nice to be in that number.

When I emailed my contact in Vermont about the restoration, he requested that I take some digital photographs and send them to him. He also suggested that I come out in the spring to fish with him during the annual mayfly hatch. He told me that he would keep me posted as to when this would be. Naturally, I agreed. After all, he is a customer!

An Accidental Fly Pattern

In the fall of 2006, my daughter took a job with a large local bank whose headquarters were in a large city on the shores of one of the Great Lakes. She moved to the warehouse district of this city to be near work. This location let her easily walk to work. She lived near the corner of two major streets and could actually see the lake from her front window. Unbeknownst to her when she rented her apartment, this lake view also ensured that she would experience the annual hatch of mayflies coming off the lake. More than twenty years ago, the lake was so polluted that there were almost no mayfly hatches. Since then the lake has experienced an increased level of cleanliness and the mayflies have come back to the downtown area to a spectacularly high extent.

One morning in late spring, she woke to an apartment with hundreds of mayflies lining her walls. She had inadvertently left open a window overnight. She called me with this emergency. She was not hysterical, as this was not her style, but I could sense the urgency in her voice.

"Dad, there are hundreds of insects all over my apartment clinging to the walls. They are everywhere," she said. "Will they bite me?" I told her about the life cycle of the mayfly, and that in the adult part of their life cycle they had no mouths. They could not bite. I told her to catch one for me to examine and use a vacuum cleaner to suck up the remainder. She did this. From then on, she used a screen in her window and never left any opening into her apartment overnight.

The first insect she sent me was about a number 18, and of course, dead when I saw it. I was somewhat disappointed in that the colors were faded. Later on that spring my wife and I had an occasion to visit her apartment, she caught a live one for me; a #14 this time, and I had a chance to study it in the light and with my magnifying lens while it was still alive. I speculated that she had been infested with a Light Cahill mayfly. The thorax was alternating light gray and dark gray circular bands, the two wings were dun color and the legs brown. I immediately decided to create a fly pattern from this fly. I have been tying flies for more than 10 years, but this was the first time that I actually studied a live insect to create a fly pattern. Usually, I reverse engineer someone else's pattern or copy a pattern from a book, magazine or website.

I selected a light gray dubbing with darker gray turkey biot quill to create the two alternating bands of light and dark gray. Dun cock feathers matched the color of the wings perfectly, and brown hackle matched the color of the legs. I decided to use dark gray thread. I tied this all on a number #14 dry fly hook. I was excited to create a fly this way and named it in honor of the person who called me early one morning in alarm, with questions about all the insects lining the walls of her apartment. So now, I was excited to have "Jen's Mayfly" added to my fly tying patterns. I could not wait to make a dozen and try them out.

I searched through my fly tying supplies and realized that I needed to order the dark gray turkey biot feather and the light fine gray dubbing to tie the fly. I called a fly fishing store, described the insect, and asked them to mail me these items. Gary, the person I talked to at the store, said that all mayflies (genus Hexagenia) have two or three tails. I said that this insect had no tails. He insisted that all mayflies have tails.

With this information, I began to doubt myself and studied the insect again. A detailed examination revealed that what I had in my possession certainly had no tails. Later that week I stopped at a fly fishing shop in a suburb of my hometown and asked the owner, George, what he thought.

"Mayflies do indeed have tails," he said. "What you have there is a midge (genus Diptera), probably a zebra midge from your description, and not a mayfly." The mystery was cleared up and I corrected the title of the pattern accordingly to 'Jen's Great Lakes Midge'. I still think that they will catch fish, no matter what I call them, and cannot wait to tie some and try them.

Lake Témmis Liar

When I arrived at the Amtrak station at about noon, there was only one employee and no customers. The passenger trains that pass through our town traveling east to New York and west to Chicago only stop in the middle of the night. I bought my ticket and looked at a large, old, yellow, faded map on the wall showing train routes all over North America. I was thinking to myself, where else could I go on a train that makes sense. One of the routes, I noticed, was from Toronto to James Bay in northern Canada.

"Does this train still run," I asked the agent pointing to the route on the map.

"Yes," he said. I picked up free copies of many train routes and schedules and filed all of this away for future reference.

Ever since I was a boy, I wanted to go fishing somewhere in northern Canada, like Lake Témmis (pronounced Te'•mis). Témmis actually exists and lies about 300 miles north of Toronto, half way to James Bay. This vague desire lay dormant throughout most of my adult life and only recently grew into an extraordinary determination; some would even say an obsession, through a series of seemingly random and unlikely events.

One of these events happened a few years ago with an ordinary business trip to Yardley, Pennsylvania. Yardley is located directly across the Delaware River from Trenton, New Jersey. At that time, the major airlines wanted $565 for a round-trip ticket from my town to Philadelphia and only $198 to Baltimore. To rent a car at the Philadelphia airport for two days would cost about $100. The regional train from Baltimore to Trenton cost $110, round-trip, and the person I was meeting in Yardley could pick me up and drop me off at my hotel. The cab fare from my hotel in Trenton to the train station would be only $5.

Therefore, my two choices were to fly into Philadelphia and rent a car at a cost of $665 or fly into Baltimore, take the train to Trenton and get a cab at a cost of $313. It was no contest; flying to Baltimore and taking the train to Trenton would save me more than half the cost. I had taken trains in Europe to travel between cities but had never done so in the U.S. This would be a first for me and I did not know what to expect.

The allotted layover time in Baltimore from the time the plane landed at the airport to the train leaving the station was about one hour. Even though I was planning to carry my bag on the plane, which would save time by not having to wait at the baggage carousel, and the fact that a shuttle bus runs every 15 minutes between the airport and train station, I was still concerned about timing. If the plane was even slightly late and I had to stand in a long line at the train station buying my ticket, I still might miss my train. Then the idea came into my head that I might be able to purchase a ticket in my hometown, or over the internet. So I made a phone call.

"Can I purchase a ticket from Baltimore to Trenton at your station?" I asked the agent at the downtown Amtrak station.

"Sure" he said, "come on down any time." So at lunch one day, I made the trip from my office to the train station to purchase my ticket ahead of my business trip. That way I would not have to wait in any lines at the Baltimore train station.

On my business trip to Yardley, I found domestic train travel to be extremely pleasurable. I rode north sitting next to the editor of editorial page for the Philadelphia Enquirer. We had a sparkling conversation about the economics of newspapers.

"We lose $10 million in annual revenue every time two large department chains merge," he told me. "I don't know how we will keep going long term when we distribute the news once a day on dead trees," he added, referring to competition from the internet. Then it was my turn to vent.

"I was the president of the board of education in my hometown and on the receiving end of some headlines and front page stories that were unfair and in some cases untrue. When retractions or corrections were printed in the next issue, they were in very fine print on page two, three or ten," I told him.

"Ha, ha" he laughed at me with delighted glee. So we spent some time discussing the biases of reporters, editors and publishers.

After conducting business in Yardley, I rode south in the seat in front of a New York U.S. Congresswoman with her chief of staff. At the time, Senators on the Judiciary Committee were grilling Judge Alito to determine his fitness for the Supreme Court. I introduced myself. Her comments about the senators, their questions and the politics of the situation were very interesting.

The train had large comfortable seats, worktables and 110 Volt AC plugs. This was important to me because I could do work on my laptop computer without worrying that my battery would suddenly die. My cell phone worked the whole way. It was morning, and the club car would make any kind of breakfast the traveler wanted. I discovered, much to my delight, that I was in love with train travel, but none of the routes from my hometown seemed interesting, convenient or worthwhile.

When I returned from my business trip and was filing my expense receipts and travel information, I suddenly remembered the route to James Bay. I could take the wilderness train to northern Canada and fly fish. I was calling this train a "wilderness" train because I saw a program on the Discovery Channel about wilderness trains. I really did not know if this train qualified as one or not. Nevertheless, taking this one to go fly fishing in Canada sounded pretty good.

"Where should I go?" I thought to myself. The train leaves Toronto at 8:40AM every day. I looked at the list of stations on the line and noticed the train stopped at Lake Témmis. This is about the same latitude as Timmons and Lake Abitibi and half way between Toronto and James Bay. The train would get there about 3:30PM. It is about a 300-mile trip.

My uncle Paul, who took me fishing when I was little, went to Lake Abitibi in Canada every year in late spring to fish for a week with a bunch of friends from the steel mill where he worked. He always timed the trip to occur after the ice broke on the lakes but before the black flies came out. To a young boy who idolized his uncle and had never been far from home, fishing in northern Canada seemed like an exotic adventure. His fishing stories always fired my imagination.

Armed with this information I checked on the internet for information about that area. I found a fishing store called Joe's Tackle Box in New Liskey. The owner's name really is Joe there.
"Say, Joe," I said over the phone, "I want to take the train to your neck of the woods, stay at fishing lodge and fly fish next spring before the black flies come out."

"Come on up," he said, "You'll be welcome. We have everything you need, but the best time to come for the fishing is exactly at the height of the black fly season." I was so disappointed. I did not want to travel that far to suffer the black flies when I could go to the mountains in Pennsylvania at the same time of the year to fish, without the inconvenience of traveling that far or putting up with the black flies.

After I hung up the phone with Joe, I started thinking. Paul always brought home a huge number of northern pike and walleye on ice in a cooler. The fishing at that time of year had to be good to excellent, but this was more than 40 years ago. Things change, or maybe Joe was lying to me and trying to extend his revenue stream by getting me to come when no one else would. But how could I find out?

First, I asked everyone I knew who fished if they had gone on a trip like this, but no one had. Next, I asked most of my acquaintances if they knew anyone who had fished in Canada. I got some responses, but when I contacted these people, no one had taken a trip like this either. I discussed the whole situation with my fishing buddy, Rodger.

"I will go with you whatever you decide to do, but just be aware that I may have other commitments the weekend you decide to go," was his response. Then I asked my daughter, if she would go with me, too.
"Sure I will go with you, but that is a busy time with all my graduate school commitments," she said. I told her that if we did not fish in Canada, we would fish in Pennsylvania as second choice.

I remembered that a few years ago, I had fished on the Grand River in Ontario. This is not nearly as far north as New Liskey but it was in Canada and a lot closer to Lake Témmis than my hometown. I had written down in my fishing journal details of this trip, including the name of the local fly fishing store, Great River Outfitters, in Ontario. I called them and explained the situation.

"Sure, go after the ice melts and before the black flies come out, why wouldn't the fish be hungry that time of the year?" said the storeowner. "But I have never made this trip either," he added. I was beginning to feel better about going, but still no one I talked to had actually made this trip. Finally, I decided that I needed to talk to someone other than Joe in New Liskey. But whom do I call? Then it dawned on me, and I decided to call the New Liskey Chamber of Commerce, where I talked to a very nice woman who answered their phone.

"The ice breaks on the lake between about May 1st and the 10th and the black flies do not appear until about June 1" she said. "These dates are not fixed, but vary from year to year depending upon the severity of the winter," she added. "Why don't you call every week to check on the progress of spring to our area of the world?"

"I will," I promised, thinking that this was wonderful advice.

"I can't vouch for the quality of the fishing though," she cautioned. So now I knew the approximate dates of the window when I could fish, but still did not know whether it would be worthwhile. Would I catch any fish?

In March of 2006, I talked to Jake Peters. He is the husband of my wife's best friend, Penny. He goes fishing in Canada via the charter airplane fly-in method. I told him the whole story.

"I can't directly help you with personal experience," he said, "but go for the adventure, whether you catch any fish or not." This sounded good. I was not exactly fooling myself. This was what I wanted to hear, and I appreciated the encouragement.

In late April of 2006, I called Mandy at the Témmis Chamber of Commerce.

"The good news is that the ice had broken, but it's still floating on the lake. There have been no boaters yet. The weather yo-yos between 9°C and several centimeters of snow," she added. This translates to about 50°F and an inch of snow. Canada uses metric weather measurements.

"I don't think the black flies will not be here any earlier than usual this year," she added.

In the spring of 2006, as I was making plans to go to Canada, other forces in my life were at work. We were anticipating the birth of our first grandchild. There were baby showers to attend in Georgia and also to be organized locally. This turned out to be the arrival of my first grandson into my fishing stories, although he was not aware of it at the time. So with all of the other activities in my life, the Canada trip was put on hold until next year. However, I was still determined to go!

Then in December of 2006, I received my bi-monthly copy of Natural Fly Fishing. I rarely subscribe to any magazine, whether fishing, news, or any other sort. I just do not have time to read them. If I subscribe to something, then the copies pile up, mostly unread, I feel guilty every time I see the stack. It is better for me not to subscribe in the first place. Natural Fly Fishing is one of the few exceptions to this rule.

There was an article in this issue about the Ottawa River Waterway. This waterway is 700 miles long, makes up a large part of the boundary between the provinces of Ontario and Quebec, and includes Lake Témmis. They even quoted Joe of Joe's Tackle Box. He told the writer of the article, "While rainbow and lake trout lurk in Lake Témmis, they aren't numerous enough to target, but the bass and walleye are plentiful." He also said, "You need a boat to reach the fish." Joe apparently was not even truthful enough to admit any of that to me. The magazine subscription paid off in an unexpected way.

Based upon this new information, I looked for my next target of opportunity. I reviewed all the stops of the Ontario Northern railway, noticed another town only a few stops short of New Liskey and would still fulfill my quest. I started looking on the internet for accommodations, places to eat, and fishing infrastructure and found a lot of information. I decided that this would be my place to target for fly fishing in the spring of 2007.

At the very end of December, I called their municipal telephone number and talked with Pat.

"The ice breaks the end of April or early May, depending upon the severity of the winter. The black flies do not come until late May or early June. There is usually a three-week window between the ice breaking and the arrival of the black flies," he said. "The fish are very hungry then, too. For more information, why don't you contact our Travel & Information Center?" He said I should call mornings in January and ask for Terry.

"We also have Don's Outdoor Store. This is the main and largest fishing store in town, and it caters to fly fishermen. We have an outfitter that rents canoes and provides accommodations, too."

All this sounded like good advice, so I immediately called Don's Outdoor Store and talked with Susan, a salesperson.

"Jim Key owns the store, but he isn't in right now," said Susan. "Here's what I know: The local lakes are full of pike, bass, walleye, white fish and lake trout. Jim is usually in mornings and can answer questions about fly fishing. We usually carry an assortment of flies. There are three places for accommodations within walking distance of the train station. We sell fishing licenses and it will cost $24.28 CDN for an eight-day conservation license. (A conservation license is about half the limit of a normal license). There are two good eating places in town, called The Garden, and The Bee restaurants. Both these places would make you a shore lunch." Now I had a lot of local information.

"A car trip from Toronto to our town would be about 300 miles and take 5¾ hours driving time," she added. "The train would take about 6½ hours, slightly longer due to the stops, but would be much more relaxing. Many townspeople take the train to Toronto rather than drive. The train also takes luggage and baggage at no additional charge for riders"

According to my GPS, the driving distance from my hometown to the Toronto Union Station parking lot is 396 miles, and a trip time of about 6½ hours.

From the Ontario Northland train website, I obtained the following information: There are daily departures both northbound and southbound except Saturday. The northbound train leaves Toronto at 8:40AM and arrives at 3:35 PM, the southbound train departs at 11:50AM and arrives in Toronto at 6:30PM. A round trip ticket would cost $161.00 CDN (2007 prices).

In January of 2007, I called the Travel Bureau in the town closest to our destination and explained my mission to Terry.
"I'll mail you some literature on accommodations, restaurants, canoe rentals and fishing," she said.

When I received the local brochure, it resembled a section of a newspaper. There were all the usual ads from local merchants, which I appreciated, and fact-style stories about local geography, history and activities. Inside she circled the best places and wrote suggestions on stick-it notes indicating this and that. It was customized to my visit and what I had told her. She wrote that while most accommodations were in town or within walking distance, almost all the places would pick us up from the train station.

"Why didn't I think of that," I asked myself. "Of course they would. This is a very small town and fisherman like me must constitute a large part of the town's annual revenue source." I decided to call this northern hospitality.

In early March 2007, I called Don's Outdoor store again and this time talked with Jim Key, the owner.

"I moved here six years ago from Minnesota and love the place," said Jim. "The ice breaks in late April or early May and the black flies don't move in until late May or early June," he added. "The best time to come is the weekend of May 18-20 and the best way to get there is by the Northlander train. It may take longer, but it may not. You may have to change trains in North Bay, but there is road construction just south of North Bay as they are enlarging the road from two to four lanes. If there is construction you could be tied up for hours, especially on popular weekends."

"You should rent a canoe from the Outfitters in town. They do not open for the season until the 2nd week of May, but send an email to their website. Dean spends winters in Pennsylvania. He will answer email to his website almost immediately. Dean may also be renting rooms. You should ask if they are going to be doing this again this year. If they are, you should reserve a room there," advised Jim. So I sent off an email to Dean.

"What about the fishing," I asked.

"The back lakes should be full of splake, rainbow and speckled trout, up to six pounds in size and at that time of year. They will 'smash' anything thrown at them," he said. "You know that 'splake' are a hybrid of speckled trout, brook trout and lake trout. They will be hitting on #12 dry caddis flies and the following size #10 and #12 nymphs: caddis, and any mayfly," he added.

"I am a fly tier," I said. "I would like to buy some flies from you right now to use as patterns. Do you want my credit card number?"

"Nah," he said. "It wouldn't be worth it from a customs point of view. I'll tell you what. I will send you a variety of patterns free. I'll put them in an envelope and mail them to you. You can pay me if you want to when you get to town or just send them back."

"How can you trust me?" I asked. "You don't even know me."

"The flies are only $1.95CDN apiece and you are a fly fisherman. It seems like a good bet," Jim responded.

"Splake can be found in Pick Lake and Lake 55, Rainbow trout can be found in Anima Nipissing River, and speckled trout in Lake 25," he told me. He pronounced the name of the river "Anima Nip."

"All these places are too far for you to hike with a canoe, but I will drive you there in my pickup truck, he offered. "My store is across the parking lot from the train station."

"Thanks for the advice," I said. "We will buy our fishing licenses and other things we need from you when we get to town."

I located the Anima Nip River on my GPS topographical map. It flows into Black Squirrel Lake, which drains into Lake Témmis through a stream whose named does not appear on my maps. It can be easily reached by car or truck on a local road. He said any number of places in town would pack us a shore lunch.

It seemed to me that a fly fishing trip for this spring was shaping up nicely. I sent all this information to Rodger and after a day or two of not hearing from him, anxiously called to see if he was available to go on those dates.

"Look, I am 79% sure that I can go," he said. Meanwhile, my daughter volunteered to accompany me if Rodger could not go.

Dean of the Outfitters called me shortly thereafter in response to my cell phone message, not the email.

"Sorry, I didn't receive your email message," he said. "We are having problems with our internet server computer and are in the middle of changing software. You can stay at my place for $100CDN per night on the nights of May 18 and 19," he added.

"That's great," I said. "We are coming by train."

"No problem," he said. "Just stroll over to my place when you get here. We won't be crowded yet at that time of year. Just send me an email confirming our conversation." I did just that.

"You can rent a canoe from me and buy a topographical map, too," said Dean. "We will be happy to take you anywhere by van for the day (and pick us up in the evening), or you could charter the plane next door for the same kind of service."

"Why don't you rent all the camping stuff you need from me and camp overnight, too?"

"I prefer a soft indoor bed this time around," I said. "We are just coming to investigate the place for future long-term adventures," I added.

"I am a fly fisherman, too," said Dean. "I can help you plan a day trip; where you could put in one spot in the morning and I would pick us up at another spot in the evening."

"That'd be great. I have a hand held Garmin GPS with installed topographical maps," I said. "That and a paper topographical map with compass as a backup should keep me out of trouble."

"You can't walk along the banks of the streams because the banks are full of overhanging trees, and bogs or swamps or all three," Dean said. "You really need a canoe to fish in those waters."

Finally, Dean asked, "Do you need a guide?"

"Not this trip," I replied. "We aren't planning on going that far."

"Well, you can get a hearty breakfast at a local restaurant. Lots of places in town will pack you a shore lunch."

"Thanks a lot for all your advice," I said.

In summary, Dean confirmed that there were many speckled (brook) trout in the Anima Nipissing River. He said that when we got there we could plan a trip with him including lodging, meals and transportation.

The flies arrived in about two weeks. There were #10 and #12 pheasant tail nymphs, a sulfur nymph, and a dry fly, supposedly a caddis. It did not look like any caddis imitation that I had seen. I immediately went to work on reverse engineering them. The first nymph, the pheasant tail, yielded to immediate inspection. In addition, I had all the materials on hand to make it. It had pheasant tail fibers, but the body (dubbing) was the color of a hare's ear nymph. The wing case was brown and there was a brown rib with cream hackles. It was not a bead head style. It was very similar to the several pheasant tail nymphs that I currently tie, but with some differences. This variant design would make a good addition to my collection.

One of the remaining two flies looked a lot like a Humphry's sulfur nymph pattern. I took both of them to the March monthly meeting of the Great Lakes Steelheader Association, a fishing club that I belong to. I attend these meetings with Rodger. Some experts there indicated what they thought the materials were in these two flies. I showed Rodger the flies and told him of my trip planning. He seemed eager to go.

In October of 2006, I had three kidney stones removed. It was very painful but not life threatening. They were crushed via lithotripsy to aid in their removal. I had one prior kidney stone in 1996 and one stone prior to that in 1985. I just assumed it was my lot in life to get kidney stones once every 10 years, and that I was now good for another 10 years. Then in February of 2007, another stone showed up, only five months later. Fortunately, I passed this one myself without surgery. I decided that I could not keep passing stones this frequently. It was interfering with my life. Something had to be done. I scheduled an appointment with Dr. Porto, my kidney doctor.

"Dr. Porto, you have to do something." I said. "Am I carrying around any additional stones that are about to cause me trouble?"

"The most recent CAT scan images you had taken were created with 1-cm wide spiral slices. Stones are generally less than 4 mm in any dimension," said Porto. "This means that kidney stones are usually too small to be seen with normal CAT scans. You will have to undergo another special CAT scan of your kidneys with 1-mm wide slices, and that that ought to do it." He explained, "One-mm wide slices means images with 10 times improvement in the resolution. Will you agree to get this scan done?"

"Sure," I said in agreement. A few days after the test I received a phone call from the doctor.

"I am looking over your CAT results," he said. There is something on some of the images, but I need a MRI to make sure. Will you get an MRI if I schedule one for you?"

I then had the MRI thinking that he was referring to kidney stones. Dr. Porto asked me to come into his office on March 30 to give me the results.

"The good news is that you don't have any more kidney stones, but the bad news is you do have a 1.4 cm cancer on your left kidney between the top and middle lobes. The CAT scan saw it, and this was confirmed by the MRI," said Porto.

"I can do the surgery via laparoscopy on an outpatient basis," he added. The surgery was scheduled for April 24. They could not schedule it any sooner. This meant that I had slightly less than four weeks between the surgery and the trip. I need to get better very quickly if I was going to make the fishing trip this year.

In early April of 2007, I had lunch with William Davis, someone whom I was counseling about his job search. I was seeing him because I donate my time to an organization, sponsored by my church, whose mission is to help others find jobs. He was a client and I was tuning up his resume.

"I am a US citizen, but I was raised in Hamilton, Ontario, as a little boy," he said, "because my father worked for a U.S. company there." Subsequently, I told him about my desire to go fishing in Canada. I also told him where it was and how I planned to get there.

To my surprise, he said, "One summer my Dad took me fishing there." He remembered that it was nice out on the lake and that there was a curfew. Boats were not permitted on the lake after dark. I was not sure how much to credit his memory. He is about 45 years old, so this particular memory was more than 30 years old. Still, this is the first person I met that was ever there.

Prior to my upcoming surgery, a physician's assistant took my medical history. I told him the story of how I ended up diagnosed with kidney cancer.

"I have been a Physician's Assistant for more than 25 years and you are one of the dozen luckiest people I have ever met," he said.

"What do you mean by that?" I asked him.

"Look," he said, "the doctors found a potentially life-threatening problem while looking for something else. There is a chance that this would have killed you before it was discovered.

"I am sure that you have heard stories of people with no symptoms for years that finally feel a pain or lump," he said. "You know the story. The surgeon opens up the patient and decides that nothing can be done. You could have been one of them."

The surgery went well, but a few days later, I landed back in the hospital with post-surgical complications. Needless to say, I did not get better fast enough to go in May. Even in June, I was still very weak from the surgery.

The good news was that the surgeon removed the entire tumor and no follow-up radiation treatments or chemotherapy was necessary. My doctor said that the cure rate was near 100% for this kind of tumor, caught this early. I decided that maybe the physician's assistant was right.

In the middle of June, I called Jim again at Don's Outdoor store. I explained to him who I was and why I did not get there in the middle of May.

"You know, you could still get there this year if you want to because in late August the flies and mosquitoes are gone but the fishing is still good," he said. "Furthermore, the air temperature should be in the low 70s. If you come then to fly fish you should use a #4 or #6 muddler minnow, streamer pattern, or any minnow imitation" he added.

I then reminded him of the flies he sent me for spring fishing.

"The dry fly I gave you is a mayfly and not a caddis fly as it said in my letter," he said. This made a lot more sense to me. He went on to describe the fly.

"The tail is very fine deer hair and the wings are rounded tip grizzle cock hackle. The other parts are peacock herl and brown turkey biot quill," he added.

I only had grizzle cock feathers that were pointed, so I stopped at a fly fishing store in the state capitol the next time I passed through and purchased the correct feather shape. I tied a few flies with all the correct materials and they actually looked better than the one Jim sent me.

Sometime in the middle of 2007, I talked with John Black about fly fishing and gave him a book on the subject. He was primarily a spin-cast tackle fisherman, but I was trying to convert him to fly fishing.

"I am willing to give it a try" John said. So we agreed to go fly fishing together in the spring of 2008.

August was a very busy time for my wife and me, and I did not get the chance to go. In late August, I received an email from the Outfitters, addressed to their email address list saying, "Thanks for a great season." So I knew their season was over.

In addition, we just found out that our daughter was graduating from a local college's Graduate School of Business with her MBA on May 18, 2008, the exact date that I would want to go next year. I guessed that the next available fishing date would be May 25 but this would be Memorial Day weekend, and May 11 would probably be too cold yet to go.

I kept thinking that there was only a narrow window of opportunity in the calendar each year, and how my life keeps conspiring against me. The more delayed this trip became, the stronger my desire to go. Why do I have this strong desire? To ease the discouragement, I tied the Canadian-style flies in my basement during the winter months while daydreaming of fishing in Canada. Naturally, a main feature of these dreams was large trout striking at the flies I was tying.

Lake Témmis Liar - Part II

In November of 2007, I was still feeling miserable from my kidney surgery the previous April. I had just had a minor follow-up surgery to remove a residual fluid filled cyst in my left kidney and was ordered to take it easy for a few days. With no work to worry about, I kept reviewing in my mind the history of my Canadian fishing quest. I was still determined to go fishing in Ontario, 300 miles north of Toronto, but had not fully recuperated from either surgery. Also, some of the mediation I was taking was producing uncomfortable side effects.

"Will I ever get there?" I kept asking myself. Finally, after adjusting my medication in late April of 2008, I felt well enough to go fishing in Canada in May. The days I had available were during the second and third weeks in May.

I had two possibilities for fishing partners for this trip. I was actually hoping that all three of us could go, but I needed at least one other person at a minimum, because the final destination was very remote and I needed a partner for safety reasons. I called Rodger.
"Say, Rodger, can you go the second or third weekend in May?" I asked.
"I'm sorry," he said. "But I'm studying for a pilot's license to fly helicopters and won't be available."
I called John Black.
"John, can you go to Canada the second or third weekend in May?" I asked.
"Yes," he responded, "but we need to go the week of May 11 rather than later in the month." Little did I know then, but he turned out to be an inspired choice as a fishing companion.

Fortunately, the ice broke on the lake that was our destination on April 27, a little early this year, so the week of May 12 would not be too soon from a weather and climate perspective. This would also permit me to attend my daughter's graduation, scheduled for the third weekend in

May. A win for all of us. Events were coming together nicely. I called Dean at the Outfitters for lodging.

"Dean, I talked you last year about accommodations, rates and meals," I said. "Do you have anything for me the weekend of May 11?" I then explained that I chose his lodge because I promised that I would make this year's arrangements with him as soon as I knew what days we were coming. Dean remembered me.

"I'm very sorry, but we have some unplanned construction going on in the lodge right now. Things are taking longer than expected to get done, so we won't be able to help you on that weekend," he said.

"Why don't you call Marge and Doug of Northland Lodge?" he suggested. This was one of the original lodges that were recommended to me so I was not concerned with this change in plans. I called Northland and talked to Marge.

"Do you have any openings at your lodge the weekend of May 11th?" I asked.

"Yes, we do" she said. She then helped me make all the arrangements. Our itinerary was very simple. On Tuesday evening, we were to leave our comfortable, suburban homes and drive to Toronto. John and I would spend the night in Toronto at some motel within a few miles of the train station so our commute would be short the next morning. We would catch the Ontario Northlander train at Toronto Union Station at 8:40AM Wednesday.

The train would arrive in Témmisami, at 3:40PM Wednesday afternoon. We would fish all day Thursday and Friday morning. We would leave the area on the southbound train at 11:50AM for Toronto, and drive until we tired. Depending upon where we were, John and I would stay overnight somewhere and get home Saturday morning.

There is a saying about the best-laid plans. Here is what really happened. The plan was for John to pick me up Tuesday afternoon at my home. We were to leave my house between 3:00 and 3:30PM. John was there on time but I was not. As I was driving home, my cell phone rang.

There was an accident on the eastbound interstate that I normally take to and from work. It took me about 1¼ hours to make the ½-hour trip from my office to home. My wife called me on my cell phone and told me about the accident and the ensuing traffic jam, but it was too late. I was already traveling on the interstate. There was no exit I could take, and I came upon a two-mile backup. As soon as I could, I took a detour, but it did not do much good. Everyone was taking the same detour. John beat me to my house and we got a late start.

John and I drove non-stop, except for gas and the border crossing, to the motel that we were staying at on the western outskirts of Toronto. John was a great traveling buddy. The entire time we were driving, we exchanged fishing stories, and discussed religion (John is a very pious man), politics and our views of life. John had not heard any of my fishing stories, nor I any of his. So just about everything I said was new to him and I was able to tell all my favorite stories once again.

Naturally, I enjoy telling fishing stories and thoroughly enjoyed the car trip. I also heard about his fishing trips to the Boundary Waters in Minnesota and to Manitoulin Island in Lake Huron. This was a good exchange. At the border, we were asked if we had anything to declare, what we were planning on doing in Canada, how long we were staying, and where we were going. John answered each of their questions. The immigration and customs agent did not ask to see any identification, and let us pass. I guess we looked mostly harmless. I felt excited just to be in Canada and observed with interest the differences in highway signs and road construction, as I usually do.

We made good time, albeit after our delayed start. The sun was shining, and John was an excellent driver. He drove the entire distance in 6 hours and 21 minutes, beating the GPS estimate by more than a dozen minutes. Of course, the GPS always utilizes the prevailing speed limits in its calculations. We ate at a local Italian restaurant. The food was good. The restaurant was close to our motel and located in an upscale area of Toronto surrounded by new multi-story residential condominiums and apartments with retail shops on their ground floors. The view of the skyline of Toronto over Lake Ontario from the restaurant at night was spectacular.

The next morning we drove to the train station on Route 2 (Queen Elizabeth Way), a main east/west highway into the city, equivalent to a U.S. interstate. Although it was only six miles away, we had to contend with rush hour traffic, which like most other big cities, includes many vehicles and very slow going. When we finally arrived at Union Station, we had to drive around the station looking for the parking garage that the GPS promised us was there. This cost us more time.

Instead, we found a local open-air lot next to the station. We were officially running late. There were thousands, if not tens of thousands of people in the train station, all hurrying to their morning destinations. They were all commuters. Later we learned that Toronto Union Station handles 200,000 passengers a day. From the size of the crowds we encountered, I believe it. We were short on time and had to battle huge rush hour crowds. We ran through the station carrying all of our luggage and fishing equipment and asked several people where we should go to catch the Ontario Northland train. No one seemed to know.

I guess that in hindsight, it should not have been surprising; given that we wanted to head to the wilderness, and everyone we talked to were big city commuters. Then we asked for directions from the local transit police. They gave us directions. We followed them almost to the end of the station where we asked a nice woman if we were on the right track. I chuckled inside, so proud that I could create a pun, even though I was worried we might miss our train.

She said, "No," and gave us a contradictory set of directions. I started to get flustered but John was one cool commuter. He said, "I will wait in the middle of the concourse with our baggage and you will go back to the police and ask them again." I followed his directions, went back to the police and they told me that we were actually on the right track, we just did not go far enough.

We did not know it at the time, but it turns out that there are two rail systems in Toronto. The commuter system, which is called "GO", and the long distance system, called "VIA". When we followed the officer's directions completely, we ended up in the "Great Hall." There was hardly anyone in it. Sounds echoed in the vast space. We quickly found the ticket agent, and bought our tickets for the Northlander VIA train.

We were in too much of a hurry to notice that there was only one ticket agent and he was not busy. The Great Hall is the original train station from a bygone era. It is vast, lit from the outside through tall beveled glass windows, and ornamented with stone columns at least three stories tall. We then went to the gate for track number 'ONE' to board our train.

All of the commuter train cars were shiny, brand new, green and white, with upper and lower passenger decks. The upper decks were like the old dome or observation cars of famous trains of the middle 20th century. What a great touch! I thought to myself, while admiring them. In my mind, I was already sitting in the upper deck watching the wilderness pass by below me. I was unconsciously smiling with satisfaction. Each train had many cars on each locomotive. One of these trains was parked on our track when we arrived at the waiting area.

Posters on the walls showed the interiors of these cars to be better than the first class sections on jet airplanes. Probably only when new, but the green and white cars all looked new to me. The gate to the track was closed and locked. A sign said to wait. We got to the gate with about 10 minutes to spare. That was cutting the timing very close, because if we missed the train, another one would not depart until the next day.

There were less than 15 people waiting for this wilderness train. While we were dressed for the wilderness (at least I thought so), we were dressed better than everyone else waiting at the gate. With only three minutes until the scheduled departure time remaining, the beautiful, new, green and white train with the upper and lower decks left the station.

As soon as it did, a short train with one locomotive, one auxiliary power unit car, two coach cars without upper decks, one dining car, a freight car, and lots of rust and chipped paint pulled up on our track at the station. The locomotive was also towing an empty, out-of-service, green and white car. The gate opened and we were herded onto the coach cars of this train.

It left the station exactly on time. It turned out that the train we caught was owned by a different railroad company than the one that owned the commuter trains. Furthermore, this railroad catered mostly to freight, not passengers. As a bonus, this was the only on-time arrival or departure of the day, or the entire trip for that matter.

The train ride was an adventure in and of itself. The gently-worn seats were slightly frayed and the passenger coach itself showed many signs of wear. It almost made me wonder if the train ride was going to be a bumpy one.

The dining car had a very limited but expensive menu. For example, a reheated hamburger cost $4.00CDN. They had a daily homemade soup for $2.25CDN. That was my favorite—although it only passes as 'fare.' Fortunately, we had brought on this trip a soft-sided cooler filled with plenty of refreshments for us to eat and drink. We were planning to consume these items in the wilderness, but discovered that they came in very handy for this leg of the trip. Most of the other passengers (who we could tell had ridden on the train more than once) brought their own food aboard. As the day progressed, the train lost more and more time compared to its original schedule.

As the train left the Toronto area, the scenery evolved from urban, to suburban, to rural. We traveled through small towns and then passed dairy farms. We saw signs of human habitation up to and through the town of North Bay. After this, the terrain changed into vast swamps, numerous unnamed lakes, and forests of pine, spruce, maple and birch with very few signs of humans.

According to local history, Europeans had not settled at our destination until 1850. That year the Hudson's Bay Company built a store on this lake. The name of the lake and the town is First Nation (Ojibwa) for "deep water by the shore."

We arrived at our destination about 5:00PM, almost an hour and a half late. It turns out this was not unusual and even expected by most people familiar with the train. In order to make up time, or more accurately not to lose any more time, the train stopped at each station for less than a minute, to pick up or discharge one or two passengers. The stop at North Bay, a major hub, lasted only five minutes. We did not have to change trains.

Only a few people got on or off at each station. At some stations, no one got on or off the train. We were on the train for 7 hours and 20 minutes. Dividing the mileage by the elapsed time gives an average speed of about 40 miles per hour. We found out later that on-time operation of this train is generally considered a joke. There is an automated message number that anyone can call to find out the actual (delayed) schedule. The Ontario Northern Railroad line operates on its own tracks and Canadian National tracks which are all generally single-line. The Northlander is usually a short train (6-8 cars normally). We were shunted onto rail sidings when any freight train needed the right of way.

And since this is their normal way of doing business, the Northlander is usually chronically late by 1½ - 2½ hours by the time it reaches the end stations northbound or Toronto southbound. On our way north the last few miles to each station always seemed to take 20 minutes. This trip we waited at sidings for two freight trains moving south. They appeared to be moving at a very high rate of speed. It must be nice to have priority.

There were very few people on the train. During the trip, I talked and made friends with Jim, the conductor, and Pete, the food service operator in the dining car. The conductor's job was to take tickets, which required little or no effort, for less than two dozen people the entire trip, and to throw the track switches when we were switched onto sidings to let the freight trains go past.

The first time he did this I was startled to look out the coach window and see him standing beside the train after an unscheduled stop. Then I realized what he was doing. He told me that the freight trains currently haul potash, sulfuric acid, gold, copper and nickel. These are all commodities. The fact that commodities are up in demand has raised prices and increased shipments dramatically.

He also said that the Canadian National Railroad sold this track and some rolling stock a few years ago to Ontario Northern because it was not profitable. Now it is a huge moneymaker – for commodities, not passengers. This is why the freight trains have precedence over passengers.

Jim told me that he was going fishing for five days himself at the end of this shift. He said he was going to Fishing Zone 13 in Quebec, Zec Restigo, and fish in Lac Bleu (Blue Lake), which is about 55 miles East North East of North Bay. Each zone apparently has slightly different fishing regulations.

He said that there is an open pit diamond mine under construction north of Moosonee (Cree Indian for "at the moose") on James Bay, the end of the railroad line. To get to the mine from the railhead, travelers have to go farther north by taking a barge in the summer or travel on an ice road in the winter.

This mine, located near Attawapiskat First Nation in northern Ontario, will be Ontario's first diamond mine. The Victor Mine will employ 400 people during production and will have an annual production rate of 600,000 carats. Victor is one of 18 kimberlite pipes discovered on the property, 16 of which are diamondiferous. The Victor kimberlite has a surface area of 15 hectares and consists of two pipes that coalesce at the surface: Victor Main and Victor Southwest. The mine will be open-pit with an expected life of 12 years and a total project life of 17 years. The De Beers Group officially opened the Victor mine on July 26, 2008.

Normal 110 Volt AC power was available in the coach cars and the dining car, so I was able to plug in my laptop computer whenever I wanted to use it. In addition, my cell phone worked in the Toronto area and whenever we passed through a town or area large enough in population to support cellular phone service. My daughter kept track of us through the schedule update phone service and called me several times during the trip, talking directly with me when my phone was in the range of a cell tower and leaving messages when it wasn't.

Jim said that "Y"s are the only places where trains can turn around, and this railroad track only has "Y"s at midpoints Washago, North Bay and Cochrane, and endpoints Toronto and Moosonee.

On the way north, I lent John one of my fishing books, Trout Madness, by Robert Traver (a pseudonym for John Voelker) to read on the trip. I brought this book along specifically for John. It is one of my favorite books written about fly fishing, and I was hoping that it would put John in a fly fishing kind of mood. He read it on the train. I am not sure how well it worked. I observed that he fell asleep several times while reading the book.

Based upon the samples provided by Jim of Don's Outdoor Store, I had tied many flies on my basement workbench prior to the trip. But since we were going so far and I had no way to replenish them or tie different flies, styles or variations, I brought my travel vice, fly tying tools and materials along to tie more flies. This is the very first time that I ever tried to do this. Since the dining car contained tables that I could attach my vice to, I tied flies there on the way north. While I was tying, I was very sensitive to the motion of the dining car and the train.

The track was not exactly in perfect shape. Railroad spikes attach the rails to the ties. The motion of the train felt like the winter freeze pulled most of them about half way out. One section of track next to a swamp had the cars leaning in that direction farther than my inner ear was comfortable with. And since we were not going around a bend, I assumed that this was not in the original track elevation plans. I did notice that we were going a lot faster than average on this section of track. I think that the engineer knew about the track conditions in this area, and his strategy to reduce the chances that something bad could happen, was to be on this tilted section of track for as short a period as possible.

It was extraordinarily difficult to tie flies while the entire car was continually swaying, shaking and rattling. It seemed like every passenger on the train eventually came by and watched for a while. They were mostly amazed at what I was doing and I ended up talking to more than half of them. While I did get more flies tied, the vice had a tendency to draw people to me, and I had a lot more friendly discussions than actual time tying on the vice.

When I commented to the conductor about the small number of passengers, he said that the train is full on weekends and holidays; and they put on extra cars for the Shania Twain (a current pop singer from northern Canada) festival, leaf tours and Christmas excursions. During the week, the trains mostly carry people going to doctors' appointments in North Bay or Toronto. It is almost mandatory to take the train in the winter because of the unpredictability and severity of snowstorms. He also pointed out that there was a modern shopping mall within walking distance of the North Bay train station and that this was not a coincidence.

The sun was shining when we left Toronto, but as the train pushed farther and farther north, the sky became more and more cloudy. Finally, it started raining at about North Bay, and was raining hard by time we reached our destination.

Doug was waiting for us at the station when the train pulled in. All total, from my home to his lodge was a 600-mile trip. We were the only two passengers that got off the train at that stop, so he knew right away who we were. He introduced himself, put our luggage in the back of his pickup truck and took us to Don's Outdoor Store, only 150 feet away. Jim, the owner had promised to keep the store open for us until the train arrived. We went in and looked around.

This store had equipment for all kinds of outdoorsmen and all kinds of fishermen except fly. John and I bought our Canadian fishing licenses. We discussed with Jim and Doug where we might go to catch trout. The consensus was the Anima Nipissing River (Nipissing is First Nation for "little water," probably in comparison to the nearby Great Lakes). I also bought a local topographical map as a backup to my GPS.

I brought along a compass and can use it thanks to the Boy Scouts. My familiarity with the compass is not really from Boys Scout training. I am actually self-taught. But as a Scout leader (troop committee), on many occasions I had to show young Scouts how to use one and help with orienteering practice. With a compass and a local topological map, I felt that I could lead us back to civilization, or our pick-up point, even if the GPS was lost or inoperable for some reason.

Our fishing day trip was to start about 19 miles out of town and we were planning to canoe three lakes, with portages between them, for a total distance of several miles through the wilderness to our pick-up point. It turned out that this was overcautious because there was a gravel road nearby. I didn't know this ahead of time. However, a first-time traveler cannot be too overcautious navigating in any wilderness area.

I had forgotten to bring my dubbing wax, an ingredient necessary to tie certain dry flies. Neither Jim nor Doug had any, so we went to a small store across the street that sold assorted tourist supplies and sundries. I bought a tube of non-flavored, non-scented Chapstick for almost triple the price at home. It worked just as well.

Although townspeople spoke Canadian English, we heard everyone using words that we did not understand. People in this area have their own private language, which required translation or at least a definition. When we asked, we learned that: Swamp Donkeys are Moose, Bush Chickens are Grouse, Mother Nature's Retreads refers to personnel in the Ministry of Natural Resources (Canadian Fish & Game Wardens) and Tundra Tuna refers to Sucker Fish. All these words are obvious candidates for entry into the Newly-Revised Canadian English Dictionary.

My experiences with local fish and game wardens were always polite and positive. Many times they came to speak at our fishing club meetings. However, the Canadians seemed to take particular delight in an adversarial relationship. I guess the fact that I never try to circumvent regulations might have something to do with our differing attitudes.

Before taking us to the lodge, Doug drove us to the local fish hatchery. He had a key and took us inside. The fish hatchery is a non-profit corporation sponsored by the local community and the Ontario Department of Natural Resources. Doug is on the board of directors. It is officially called the "The Fish Involvement Program" The hatchery building was located between Lake Airways and Outfitters directly on the lake. The hatchery was surprisingly small.

We toured the hatchery, both rooms. The front room was an office. In the back room, 1.2 million walleye eggs were hatching. The intention is to put the hatched eggs (called fry) into local lakes. This part of the hatchery consisted of eight vertical clear plastic pipes about six inches in diameter and six feet long. Each was filled with lake water and about 150,000 fertilized eggs. Fertilized eggs do not float, and were supported by a screen within the water column about chest high. The egg columns require fresh lake water to be constantly circulated through them. The cold lake water was bubbled up from beneath the eggs agitating them and providing oxygen. The overflow water from the top of the columns ran off through a screen, so no eggs or fry could accidentally escape, back into the lake. And, although there was no burglar alarm on the facility, there was an elaborate alarm system to telephone responsible parties if the water flow stopped.

Lake Airways is a charter airline, and is located in the building next to the hatchery. It has one "Beaver" floatplane that flies two to three round trips a day to ferry fishermen to even more remote locations. Officially, the name of the plane is a De Havilland Canada DHC-2 Beaver. This plane was designed in 1946 specifically as an eight-place bush airplane by De Havilland Canada. The Beaver is still considered a classic workhorse. It is powered by the Pratt & Whitney R-985 radial engine of 450 hp. The Beaver is still used in large numbers throughout Canada, Alaska, and in other remote areas of the world. One of the major reasons they are still in service is that no comparable replacement has ever been marketed. The sound it makes on takeoff is very distinctive. No one who has ever heard it is likely to forget it. It was the only airplane we saw or heard the entire time we were in the area. There were no contrails in the sky either. The pilot can put a canoe on one of the pontoons to take this along too. Lake Airways charges $600 and up per round trip.

Doug then drove us to his home, which is also the lodge. It is named Northland Lodge. It was only about 500 yards from the center of town. His lodge is on a linked chain of five lakes. Altogether, there was more than 100 miles of shoreline. We met Marge, his wife, who is the cook and housekeeper for all the guests, and Bud, their dog.

There are two buildings on his property, a main lodge and an outbuilding. The lodge parking lot is between them. The outbuilding has six guest suites, three up and three down. The main lodge has three levels, and between 3,000 and 4,000 square feet of space. The top level consists of two spacious apartments. We had one and a local family of eight was using the other. They had been "renting" it for one month. They were having a house built and it was late in completion. They had to be out of their first house by the middle of April, so they needed a place to stay until the middle of May. They were a husband and wife with six children, the oldest about 11. Marge charged them the first week's rent and then forgave the last three weeks. The husband began helping Doug by doing chores around the lodge and they gave back the first week's rent, too.

I could sense that Marge was not very happy with all the kids around and no rent money, but the kids loved Doug and one little girl had become attached. At bedtime, she had to hug Doug good night. The kids were all extremely mannerly and very well behaved.

Doug owns a small fleet of five identical aluminum boats with nine horsepower motors. He also owns a dozen canoes, some aluminum and some Kevlar, and a mobile canoe rack that can be pulled by his pickup truck. This rack holds at least eight canoes.

We took our luggage and fishing equipment up to our rooms on the upper level. Since we were already late, we had to hurry along. We had a bathroom, a kitchen with dining room, a living room, one bedroom with two twin beds, and one bedroom with a double bed. The living room had a twin bed in it, a rollaway bed and a sofa. I guess that it could sleep six. The kitchen had a stove, refrigerator, dish cabinet with dishes, pots and pans.

Doug is a tall man, well over six foot tall and just shy of 60 years old, with a tanned face, large and calloused hands, thinning white hair, a mostly white beard and mustache, and ready smile. He habitually wears an old baseball cap with "Northland Lodge" embroidered on it, and is a ready storyteller. He told many stories, and must have told these same stories for many years, because they were all smoothed, polished, and of course, slightly exaggerated at all the right spots. You might say that it takes one to know one. He wore old clothes and work boots, something he was exceeding proud of, as he pointed this out to us several times.

Doug's primary job is to own and run the Northland Lodge. He acts as a fishing and hunting guide, too, when necessary. He does a few other things to supplement this income that I will discuss later. His wife does all the cooking and cleaning for all the apartments and guests. She hangs all the bedding out to dry on a clothes line mounted on pulleys between the two buildings. She does not make guests beds each day or clean the room while you are out fishing like a hotel maid would, but does the laundry and cleaning between customer stays.

We had dinner Wednesday evening at the lodge. Marge cooked ham, scalloped potatoes, two kinds of salad, hot beets, a loaf of homemade bread, and for dessert, homemade blueberry and red raspberry pies. When Marge remained in the kitchen after serving us, I invited her to sit and eat with us. She replied that she does not eat with Doug and his clients but always eats earlier. The food was fabulous. After diner, what I did was an easy decision; I helped Marge clear away the dinner dishes. I also helped her in the kitchen. I felt uncomfortable when Marge served us but did not join us.

After dinner, John and I sat with both Doug and Marge and talked for several hours. I was glad that I could persuade Marge to join us. These hours were a fascinating glimpse of life in the north of Canada. For example, in response to a question about local industry, Doug said the only industry left in town is tourism. The Shera Mine, just north of town, was an open pit type mine for iron ore but closed several years ago. There is no lumber mill in the town either. There are quite a few fishing and hunting lodges in the area to accommodate tourists, like us.

The town residents are aware of what is going on in the outside world. Virtually everyone has satellite TV reception, including Doug and Marge, so they can watch all the same nightly news and television shows that can be seen in Toronto, and on all the States networks. They are limited in their internet connections. Apparently, the only available (public) internet connection is at the public library. Townspeople can use it free; out-of-towners have to pay.

Doug says he has been featured in many outdoor magazines, and when the Ontario Ministry of Natural Resources (MNR) holds a conference for outdoor writers, they ask Doug to host some of them. He showed me some magazines with articles about him in them. He said that one time a group of writers came up for a three-day expedition in the spring and spent the entire time in the lodge while it snowed. Doug said he provided them with local commentary.

He said the Ontario MNR is a poor payer, and that it ends up costing him money whenever they promise to pay for Province guests expenses. He says he does it anyway. I asked if he gets any increased clients that way. He says he doesn't think so, but has no way to really know. He says that the same regulars come up about the same time every year.

He told us that he was a featured speaker at an annual fur trapper conference a few years ago. He described about how he cooks wild game and other recipes. He said that he received many email responses from that talk from as far away as Minnesota and Manitoba. Doug told us that he would like to do a television show about cooking wild game and fish. He has thought about lining up sponsors, mostly companies that sell winter outdoor goods.

Doug said that the town has about 300 residents. The official count is near 1000, but that includes many outlying areas. The population density works out to be less than half a person per square kilometer.

I noticed that the tables and chairs, walls and ceilings were all made of pine. The dining furniture all looked homemade. I suggested that he could take some time in the winter months and with maple and birch being so plentiful, he could make some beautiful furniture. He said that they routinely burn veneer quality maple and birch – and use pine for furniture and put it on the walls and ceilings precisely because you cannot burn it in your furnace.

Doug said that he burns 25 cords of maple and birch wood each winter. He cuts and splits his own fire wood from designated "clear cut" property. Each year the Province sells licenses to cut and remove firewood from certain tracts of land. The normal course of events is to take more firewood than the license allows. Firewood is permitted to dry for two years. So in the spring of 2008 he is cutting wood to burn in the winter of 2009-2010. He already has his wood cut and drying for the winter of 2008-2009.

We started talking about local customs and what the differences were between his town and Toronto. Doug says that they do not lock any doors and he leaves his ignition key in his pickup truck in case someone needs to borrow it. He has no worries that it will be stolen. However, he says that a pile of firewood would be stolen in 10 minutes if no one were looking. People also steal live fish from lakes to put them in other lakes.

Other than that, there is no theft. We were not given a key for our rooms, even though it had an outside entrance. Only on the last day when we were giving our rooms one last look, checking for forgotten items, we discovered a key hanging on some hooks. It looked like it had not been used in a long time. Nothing was touched or taken.

Doug told us that he mostly lives off the land. He hunts in the fall, traps fur animals in the winter, fishes in the summer and only eats wild game and fish. He gathers wild berries, and wild fruit, such as plums, when in season. He cans sucker fish, corn, peaches, green beans, pickles sweet and dill, relish, plum, blueberry, pear, peach, onions and asparagus.

Bushels of some fruit, like peaches, come from friends in the Niagara region. He has a large walk-in pantry with rows of shelves filled with hundreds of full quart jars. He has a large pressure canner, which he places on their kitchen stove. He says that this provides sufficient heat for pressure canning. He says that this is the fastest way to preserve food. He also has three deep chest freezers, filled with moose, muskrat, sausage, partridge, beaver and rabbit meat.

He plants vegetables on the southern side of his house, including many different kinds of spices such as parsley, and lemon basil. Tomatoes cannot really be grown this far north. If someone were to plant them, they only get yellow but not red because it is never gets warm enough. Any gardener would have to pick them and take them into the house to ripen.

In the summer, he leads groups on half-day tours of old growth forests and of orchards and other wildflowers. He charges $100 per tour.

Every winter he runs a trap line on provincial property. He skins all the animals that he catches, processes their meat, and dries pelts – fox, rabbit, mink, raccoon, muskrat, beaver, bear, and red, gray and black squirrels.

The snow pack in winter averages five feet. He visits his traps twice a week on a snowmobile. The animals are always dead and frozen solid when he finds one in a trap. There are no deer or turkeys in the forests around town. It is too cold for them to survive. He picks up all road-kill. The local police call him when they find some and he comes and picks it up. He processes this meat. It was not clear whether he keeps this meat or shares it. I suspect the latter. He does meat processing for everyone in the town.

In an average winter, low temperatures are typically -30° F to -20° F. Highs are up to 0° F. One cold January a few years ago, the high was less than -40° F for one month straight. When temperatures reach the 40s to 60s, townspeople wear shorts, T-shirts, and flip-flops, because it feels warm to them. John and I were wearing our coats, flannels, or sweatshirts, especially in the evenings, while the townspeople were only wearing t-shirts.

The school in town is for grades 1-8. It has 135 students, who are drawn from very large surrounding area. The closest high school is 60 miles to the north. The local school year starts in early September and goes through June 25. The students have many vacation days, such as around Christmas, Easter, national holidays, and of course, snow days, when it is too cold or storming so badly that the buses cannot move.

Doug and his wife live a combination entrepreneurial, communal and pastoral lifestyle. He treats other people very well. He freely shares what he has, for example, letting the temporarily homeless family live for one month in the rooms upstairs practically free. He waves to everyone in town and they wave back. Doug says you can always tell an outsider because they do not know to wave at everyone. He charges clients from out-of-town for room and board and services, and everyone in-town for the use of his log splitter, meat processing, or animal skin drying, etc. but apparently only if they can afford it. He sells his furs in North Bay.

Before Doug became a lodge owner, he was a truck driver for 19 years. He has owned this lodge for the last 18 years. He worked for a Toronto trucking company that hired him out. His claim to fame is that for many years he drove Bruce Springsteen on tour. His greatest thrill, however, was that he met Bob Seeger (of the Silver Bullet Band fame) backstage at a Springsteen concert. He claimed that when he was a truck driver, he spent 75% of his money on women and booze, the rest he wasted.

When the discussion got around to how he met and married Marge, he said that he blew in her ear and she followed him to town. And Marge said, "Yes, that was exactly what happened." He does not drink or smoke now and said he quit 30 years ago. He said he loved top-shelf Scotch whiskey. After this declaration, I felt that I should not tell him about my collection of very old single malt Scotch. Alcohol costs much more in Canada than in the US. So just before we left for Témmisami, I asked him if I could bring him any alcohol either duty free or from across the border. He said no, thus further confirming his status as a non-drinker. But he did say he could use an 8-weight fly reel.

The local population and tax base are not sufficient to support a police force on its own, so it uses the Ontario Provincial Police. Each homeowner is taxed about $90CDN per year. This is not enough revenue to support these services so the balance of the money comes from the Ontario Provincial Government. The police have an office on the main road in town. There is little or no crime. This service does not cover First Nation policing. The Anishinabek Police Service is located in North Bay and provides policing services for individual First Nations that are located nearby in the Province of Ontario.

A few years ago, Doug was president of the Chamber of Commerce. He said that he came up with the idea to renovate the local fire tower, and for an annual fall wild game dinner and auction. Townspeople called all of these things "just another one of Doug's crazy ideas." The Chamber wanted to charge for the dinner to raise money, but discovered that this is against some Canadian law about the sale of cooked food, so they could not serve dinner. John immediately suggested that they say on the advertisements that the dinner is free but there is a charge for the auction. Doug was amazed and liked this idea very much.

Doug said that to raise money for the auction he asked their local Minister of Parliament to donate something for the auction. The Minister provided a red tie worn by a former Prime Minister Pierre Trudeau, who was Prime Minister from 1968-1979 and 1980-1984. Among other things, he was flamboyant and famous for wearing red ties. The tie was accompanied by a letter from Trudeau addressed to Doug Adams attesting to its authenticity. Because the letter had his name on it, Doug kept bidding against his friends (who were bidding up the price to torment him). They finally let Doug pay $245CDN for the free tie and accompanying authenticity letter he solicited.

Doug said that he was on the town council when they started the fish hatchery. He is now on the hatchery board of directors. That is why he had the key and was so proud to show it off to us.

Doug said that there are no secrets in a small town, and pretty much everyone in town knew who we were and that we were his lodge guests.

I showed Doug and his wife my fly rods and reels. We then showed each other our respective fly collections. Marge was fascinated to know that I personally tied all of the flies that I showed them. Neither Doug nor Marge knew how to tie a fly, nor apparently did anyone else in town that they knew.

Finally, I said that I had brought my fly tying equipment with me. Marge asked me to show her how I tied a fly. I tied a mayfly for her. She couldn't believe that it was only one continuous strand of thread. I gave her the fly and she asked for the name of the manufacturer of the vice and the names of the tools I used. I promised to send them to her.

Doug then took us on a tour of his house. On the main level were Doug and Marge's private rooms, the main kitchen, the dining room, and the living room with large windows facing the lake. There were two apartments on the upper level. We were staying in one of them. The lower level contained a large game room with a pool table and shuffleboard game, a sauna, a wood burning furnace, a meat processing room complete with stainless steel sinks, tables, and band saw, a wood shop, a metal shop, a fully equipped garage for snowmobiles, and the pantry. The lower level also contained three chest freezers, the electrical panel, and the city sewage system. Doug has city water and city sewage. The lower level leads directly out to the lake. All of the firewood for the winter of 2008-2009 was already stored under the main "living" level porch. Doug also stored all of his boating paraphernalia in this area.

The central and most revered object on the lower level is the wood burning furnace, which burns maple and birch and heats whole house. This is supplemented with electric baseboard heat when necessary. There was a door in the basement at the entrance to the stairs, which led to the main living level. The stairwell was enclosed and a high power fan was built into the wall above the doorframe, which pushed warm air up the stair well to the living level. The heat in the living level warms the floors in the upper level. I realized that Doug had created a homemade "forced air" heating system without needing air ducts.

Doug loved to tell his stories. I went through three phases of listening. At first, I was enthralled with the stories. The second phase was one of boredom and annoyance. The third phase was the most fun. I actively listened, and then asked subtle questions illustrating the ridiculousness of the claims and exaggerations, which lead to the point or the moral of the story. This give and take became a game between us. He was a master and I learned much from him.

I noticed a large collection of religious books above a built-in desk near the kitchen. It was not obvious. I asked about them. It turns out that Marge is a two-Sundays-a-month minister. She preaches alternate Sundays opposite a paid traveling minister at the Anglican (Episcopal) Church in town. This denomination is the sole representative in Canada of the worldwide Anglican Communion. Their church is in the Diocese of Algoma, based out of Sault Ste. Marie. I found out later that Marge is an ordained lay reader in the Anglican Church although she did not say so at the time. She also runs a Bible study for the women in the town, regardless of denomination. She has no divinity degree but a lay reader's ordination requires approximately 1½ years of study under the tutelage of someone who is an ordained minister in the Anglican Church. She received a certificate signed by the local bishop when she was ordained. She mostly follows an Anglican preaching annual, but none of the reference books on her desk were even remotely new.

For such a small town Marge has competition. There is also a United Church of Canada and a Roman Catholic Church in town. The United Church is the largest protestant church in Canada. It was formed in 1925 when the Methodist, Congregational, and 70% of the Presbyterian churches merged to form one denomination. Several other denominations have joined it since. I suspected that Marge, as a part-time minister of God, was either a volunteer or very poorly paid staff member.

I told her of my experiences as a Presbyterian elder and worship leader. I also told her that I attended an Anglican Communion service at King's College Chapel at Cambridge University in England a few years ago, what it was like to hear the organ and the boys' choir, and experience that service. I told her a sign on the organ said that King Henry the VIII donated it about 1543. I also said that I had visited Westminster Abbey more than four times. She could not believe that someone sitting in her dining room, who was not even an Anglican, had been to two of the Anglican churches most revered places of worship.

I have a modest collection of about two to three dozen worship leader books that I accumulated over the years and use. God must have been whispering in my ear, because I immediately understood that I was to send her some of the pastoral books from my bookshelves. I rationalized that I could always buy new ones. I wanted this to be a surprise to her so I did not tell her about my decision. John is a devout Roman Catholic and I could not have made the trip without him, so the three of us comprised an ecumenical bunch. Later, I wondered about the strange and unnatural chain of events that sent us to their lodge rather than to the Outfitters. Now if John and I were supposed to be doing the Lord God Almighty's work on earth, surely He would provide at least a few fishes! Marge provided all the homemade loaves.

The church that Marge leads used to have an oil-fired furnace, which was only turned on for services. The remainder of the time the church was left cold to save money. In addition, she said the furnace was so old that many parishioners felt that it would explode at any time. So in 2008 they bought a propane furnace for $1,000CDN. The only problem is that propane gas turns to jelly at about -35°C. Sometimes it gets colder than that in the winter!

We noticed that there are numerous very-large exposed rocks in the area. Doug said that most of the local rock is granite, but there are also nickel, copper and sulfur bearing ores and magnetite, which is iron-bearing in the area. The rocks in the area are both volcanic and sedimentary. This area is in what is known as the "greenbelt" of rock formations. As a side effect, the high iron content of the magnetite ore under town and in the area prevents cell phones from working. The locals all know which street corners and other spots around the town have cell phone reception.

A word needs to be said about Bud, the third member of the lodge staff. He has been with Doug and Marge for many years and is treated like a member of the family. He is the official lodge greeter. When he is not sleeping in the middle of the front door (outside) or in the middle of a room (inside), he follows Doug around. Bud is a large, friendly, light yellow colored dog, half Labrador retriever and half husky. With this ancestry Bud could be the picture in the encyclopedia entry for "very large dog." Doug said that the only protection Bud offers to the lodge is that he could lick an intruder to death. Marge added that he also sheds his fur year round, not just in the spring. As large as Bud is, he must have been kept inside the lodge with constant human contact when he was a puppy and a young dog, because he still thinks that he is a lap dog. If anyone sits on the couch in the living area, he joins you.

A representative of a major, high quality manufacturer of fly-fishing equipment stayed at their lodge last year and gave a very expensive, brand new, 8-weight fly rod to Doug when he left. He also left the fly line and backing, but Doug had no way to use it without the reel. The first night at the lodge, I bartered Doug a used 8-weight fly reel for some mink, red, black, and gray squirrel, and fox fur. I intend to use this fur to tie some flies.

Marge and I discussed cooking and recipes. I told Marge that I have a recipe for English scones and that many of them do not survive the cool-down to room temperature when my family is around. She said that she wanted the recipe for any scones with that reputation. She said she couldn't make good Scottish shortbread either, although she had tried several times. I promised to send her some recipes that could not fail.

When we arrived, the Canadians were just heading into major four-day weekend. Friday was schoolteacher development day and Monday was Victoria Day. No one I asked knew what Victoria Day celebrated. I later found out that Queen Victoria's birthday was celebrated on May 24, now this fixed holiday is the birthday celebration of the (any) current reigning monarch. It is still called Victoria Day in her honor. She reigned from 1837 to 1901, and to this day is still the longest reigning monarch, although Queen Elizabeth is approaching her record.

Before we went back to our apartment, Doug asked me what kind of canoe we wanted for our trip tomorrow. I had the choice between an aluminum canoe with wide flat bottom and a Kevlar canoe with a deeper keel. I chose the Kevlar, not only for the lighter weight, but because with a deeper keel, we could more easily hold a line against or across any wind direction. Flatter bottomed boats are more easily pushed by the wind across the surface of a lake. John and I went to bed about 11:00PM, exhausted by the day's events.

John set his alarm and we got up at 5:30AM. I took some wonderful digital pictures of the lake at dawn. The water pressure in the bathroom was very weak, although the water was very hot. We went down to the dining room and had breakfast at 6:00AM. Marge cooked homemade scratch biscuits, eggs any way you wanted them, thick slices of bacon, homemade preserves, juice, coffee, tea, fresh strawberries, blueberries, homemade muffins and toast. We learned the berries were from hot houses in Canada in the Niagara region.

For our first day of fishing, Doug loaded a Kevlar canoe in the back of his pickup truck. We took Highway 11 north and then turned west on Black Squirrel Lake Road. This was a logging road, and went directly through Anishinabek (Native Indian) territory. The Anishinabek (Ojibwa) have been living in the area for at least 6,000 years after migrating from the east coast of North America. The put-in site was about 19 miles from the Northland Lodge.

Black Squirrel Lake road was built with crushed rock from the side of the road. The logging company who maintains the road does not bring in loads of crushed rock from elsewhere to make the roads. They use black powder to blast out the local rocks and bring in a mobile rock crusher to make the rock gravel right on the spot where it is needed. Coarser crushed rock makes the base and finer gravel the surface of the road, which crunched under Doug's truck tires.

I had loaded (digitally) the local topographical into my hand-held GPS. It worked flawlessly. The map on the screen was extremely congruent to the geographical features we could see. I was amazed at how the product engineers could do this so accurately, even in the wilds of Canada. As an experiment, I moved from the right side of the road to the left and back again. The little arrow on the GPS's screen followed me perfectly. The GPS indicated that it was tracking 9 to 10 satellites and said that it knew where I was to an accuracy of ± 15 feet. I believed it!

Doug dropped us off at a pool of the Anima Nip River, right where my GPS said he should. The put-in point was the stream from McLean Lake that emptied into the Anima Nip River. This water flowed under the road through three huge culverts. The water was pouring at a very high rate into the Anima Nipissing River. No doubt, the impressive flow rate was caused by spring runoff from melting ice and snow. Doug helped us carry our canoe and all our equipment into this flow. When we sat in the canoe and pushed off, the canoe shot out into the current and we had a few tense moments keeping the canoe upright and avoiding the rocks. As soon as we got into the main river pool, everything became much easier.

The water table was very high. The water was gin clear. I estimated that we could see down at least 10 to 12 feet. The air was clean with absolutely no pollution. The greens were all the new green colors of spring. It felt like the world was new again. Maybe this is not so far off the mark. The land and people had just come out of eight months of deep, hard winter. Everything in nature was waking up and you could feel it.

We paddled to the entrance of the first pool, strung up our rods and began to fish. I gave John my 6-weight graphite fly rod with a mid-arbor reel, and I chose a 4-weight because I felt that the 6-weight was a much more forgiving setup for John to learn on. The 4-weight is sometimes a much more technically difficult tackle to use, especially in windy conditions. I was very excited and expected a lot of action. There were no insects in the air at this time of day and no visible rises, so I chose to use wet nymphs to start.

A "rise" or more properly called "rise ring" are the concentric ripples of water that propagate outward from the spot on the surface of a body of water where a trout takes an insect. This ring is usually created when the trout's lips and/or mouth break the surface of the water, as they suck in their food.

I was not worried about the number of fish we would catch. There was little or no wind and the air and water temperature were good. Fishing conditions were as near perfect as you could get. We fished the inlet of the pool to the far end and back again with no hits. We paddled close to the rapids, fished these, and then let the current push us across the pool. We fished every corner of the pool with no hits. I estimate that we fished about two hours in the pool with no luck.

The outlet of this pool of the river was a series of rapids down to the next pool of the river. This was not navigable by us in the canoe. The only way was to portage. At this point, we could not believe how bad our luck was. At about 9:30AM insects started appearing in the air, but there were no rises. Were there any fish in this pool? After two hours of fishing, with no rises and no hits, John and I decided to try the second pool.

We initially assumed that the way into the pool was also the way out, and this may have been possible when water flow rates were normal. However, the very high flow rate precluded us from getting out the way we got in. We put into shore just downstream of the inlet from McLean Lake. I got out of the canoe and started moving up the hill towards the road. I climbed to the road with no sign of a trail that I was looking for. That is when I spotted it, only five yards from where we landed the canoe.

Here was a portage path for the canoes, although, the portage path looked like it may have not been used yet this year. I wondered at that fact that I didn't spot this path from no more than 15 feet way as I made my way back up the hill. I followed the path back down to the river and called to John to tell him about it. He brought the canoe over and we proceeded to pull the canoe up the slope. It was difficult work. We scouted ahead along the road and left a marker on a bush that was near the entrance to the portage trail down to the second pool. We didn't want to miss the trail and have to backtrack carrying a heavy canoe. We then carried the canoe about 100 yards along the road until we came to the marker to the second pool. We stopped several times to catch our breath and switch aching hands that gripped the canoe. When we stopped, we could hear the river making noise over rocks and through the rapids between the pools. I realized that this must have been what Lewis and Clark experienced, although I really knew that civilization was not too far away, and we were not carrying two years of supplies.

We put the canoe in at a spot in the second pool near the rapids and began fishing again. I brought a few extra and different fly patterns along, just in case. At this point, we tried every one of them, one after another, with no response from the trout. By now, I wished I had brought an even larger assortment. We fished at the base of the rapids, anticipating that trout would normally congregate here due to the aeration from the rapids. We then spent the next two hours fishing the entire length and breadth of this pool with no hits. We saw some insects but there were no rises. We saw no fish, nor did we see anyone else fishing on these lakes. At noon, we decided to have lunch and then go to the third pool.

We picked a steep place on the shore to pull out. John was in the bow and got out of the canoe first. He then proceeded to pull the canoe out of the water. In order to pull the canoe up the rather steep slope, John gave a more than normal tug. Unfortunately, the canoe decided to tip over. I attribute this accident to a freak of nature and not John. I fell in the river only three feet from shore. The water was very cold and my feet did not touch bottom. The depth of the river was over my head this close to shore. By measurement, the water temperature was 54°F although it felt a lot colder.

I grabbed the life preserver in one hand and the canoe in the other. Fortunately, John managed to quickly upright the canoe and I was almost the only thing that went over the side. While I am slightly overweight, John's jokes about me being "top heavy" were not appreciated! I was soaked in very cold water up to my neck. The canoe got some water in it as well, which soaked a good many items. I managed to get to shore by holding onto the canoe and pulling myself out while John held the canoe steady. Again, John was very "cool under fire" and knew exactly what to do. I was so glad he was with me. When I climbed to shore, I helped John pull the canoe the rest of the way up the slope.

John and I got all the items out of the canoe and tried to keep those items that did not get wet from getting wet now. I was wearing four layers over my upper body. I took off everything above my waist and asked John to lend me one of his layers. Fortunately, my North Face jacket, which was near the front of the canoe, was dry. With one of John's sweatshirts and the jacket, my upper torso was warm. We hung all of the wet clothes I had taken off on branches on the side of the road to dry in the sun. The air temperature was 62°F so at least I would not freeze. Doug was not scheduled to pick us up for three more hours.

I had enough canoeing experience to know to seal (against water) the items that needed to stay dry. The good news is that all of my waterproof pouches worked. This preserved everything in a dry state, including my wallet, cell phone, camera and fishing book. Nothing floated away or sank. The GPS got wet but, fortunately, it's waterproof.

To dry off my pants as much as possible, I sat on a rock in the sun. Marge had made us a shore lunch, which included ham sandwiches with a ½-inch thick slice of ham, lettuce, mustard and tomato. I also brought along apples and drinks. We sat down in the sun to eat lunch. The food was delicious.

After sitting still while eating, my teeth began to chatter. I was feeling cold from the waist down. My toes felt like they were ice cubes. I told John I was beginning to feel really cold. John got me up and insisted that we walk up and down the road to warm me up. Thank God for John's common sense. We did this three times. We saw some moose droppings on the road, but no moose. We saw several cars pass on the road, no more than 100 yards away, and waved, but did not ask any of them for help. Finally, my pants dried and I felt warm enough to continue the fishing that we came for in the first place.

Twice during the day we heard the Lakeland Airways Beaver floatplane pass overhead or nearby. He must have been ferrying passengers or freight north of town.

At the pickup point, we fished from shore for a while and Doug arrived precisely at 4:00PM. He had been cutting fire wood all day. We explained what happened and that we had no luck. He then drove us to Lake 55, which was also on Black Squirrel Lake Road and told us to try there. We fished another hour and a half with no luck. We did see a black female mink on the shore of Lake 55. We saw 17 suckerfish about 13-14 inches long in Lake 55, near the outlet of the lake.

When Doug picked us up from Lake 55, we met a Canadian fisherman from Niagara Falls, who was there for the week. He was a spin fisherman and had caught nothing. Doug checked around town while we were fishing on Lake 55 and discovered that no one else was catching anything either.

On the way back to his lodge, Doug drove us to the fire tower, which sits on the top of Caribou Mountain. A sign said that visitors had to pay $3CDN to go up the tower, but we just followed behind Doug. I felt slightly guilty about this, but there was no place to pay. There was a local museum at the fire tower's parking lot, but it was closed. I guessed that we were out of season (early). The elevation of the top of the tower is 1,368 feet. We climbed the tower and took pictures of the surrounding lakes and the town. We saw some birds of prey circling the tower and rising on thermals around the mountain.

Marge cooked an enormous dinner for us, including a large steak each, and moose roast if we wanted some, baked sweet potatoes, two salads, homemade scratch biscuits, and fresh baked berry pies with ice cream. The food was fabulous. I tried a few mouthfuls of roast moose and it was good. It seemed very lean and tasty.

That evening we helped Doug put his boats in the lake for the year since he was expecting 15 guests for the four-day holiday starting the following day. John and I helped Doug load one of his aluminum boats, a 9-horsepower motor, and a gas can into the back of his pickup truck for tomorrow's fishing. I can't explain exactly why John and I always pitched in and helped. We were paying guests, but it seemed so natural to help with the chores whenever we could. We also watched Doug split some firewood with his gas-powered hydraulic log splitter. He said that he bought it for $2,000CDN, uses it himself and rents it out for about $25CDN per day to anyone else who wants to use it.

After dark, on the dining room table, Doug and I studied my topographical maps, discussed strategy and decided to go to Lake 25 the following day. We made plans for Doug to go with us as our guide to help us catch some fish. At the beginning of the trip, I was confident that I knew how to catch trout. However, some of this confidence eroded with the lack of success on the Anima Nip River and Lake 55 earlier in the day. I wondered if there was some trick to catching local Canadian trout that I did not know, but could learn from Doug. Asking Doug to go along seemed like cheap insurance to catch some fish on this trip.

We were tired and went to bed early that night. It was warm in our apartment so I opened the French doors to the lake. It was very peaceful.

We were up at 5:30AM. Again, I took digital photographs of dawn over the lake. Breakfast was at 6:00AM, with the same menu as the day before. Why mess with perfection? I felt that I needed all the calories, carbohydrates and protein as fuel for some strenuous daily activities.

After breakfast, Doug drove us and his boat and motor to Lake 25. The road to this lake was not maintained like Black Squirrel Lake Road. It was full of potholes and the truck could only go a few miles per hour. I asked Doug about shocks, struts, springs, tie rods, etc. He said that the local garage does a land office business in repairs and that vehicles are always being repaired.

We put the boat in the water and Doug mounted the motor. Lake 25 was much larger than Lake 55 or the Anima Nipissing River pools. I was glad we had a motor to get to the fishing spots. Doug fished with us and acted as our guide. He knew where all the good spots were on the lake, and where the fish were most likely to hide. I could tell from my limited knowledge of trout behavior that he was a professional at this.

One thing was apparent though, Doug did not know how to cast a fly line. He spent his time standing up in the boat and letting his line smack the water on his front cast and on his back cast. He had too much line out; much more than he could easily control. Maybe he was trying to impress us with the length of his casts, or maybe he thought that he was a tournament distance caster, but this is a rooky mistake.

The lake was completely silent and the sound of his line hitting the water almost sounded like a gun going off. On each of his casts, I cringed as his back cast hit the water, SPLAT, and on the front cast, his line hit the water, SPLAT. So when he cast his line, it sounded like SPLAT-SPALT-pause, SPLAT-SPALT-pause, SPLAT-SPALT-pause. If this is not a great way to put down wary trout, I do not know what is. He apparently did not know to use false casts to extend the length of his line without touching the water.

It has been my experience that using stealth to approach wary trout and making shorter and more accurate casts is much more productive than longer less accurate and noisier casts. Since it was his boat and his expertise we were relying on to get us to the best fishing spots and show us where the fish normally hide, I felt ambivalent about telling him his technique was lousy. He was guiding us pretty much as a goodwill gesture and not as a $250 (or more) per day guide. We ended up paying $50CDN for his boat and gas.

Most of Canada had been clear-cut in the past but there were a few stands of old growth forests in the area. Old growth forests have trees that are 300-400 years old. This was a tourist attraction for the town. These trees are not as large as giant redwoods for example, because of the short growing season this far north, but they are old. Doug pointed out one pine tree on Lake 25 that was old growth. This fascinated me and I took several pictures of it. Imagine a tree that was older than the American Revolution, or the landing of the Pilgrims, or was a sapling when Samuel de Champlain sailed up the St. Lawrence River and founded Quebec (July 3, 1608). The wonder of it boggled my mind.

We saw a beaver dam and the beaver's lodge at the outlet of the lake. There were piles of tree branches about 3-4 feet long under the water near the beaver lodge that looked like they were stripped of their bark. Doug said that this was the beaver's food supply. We did see some small fry jumping out of the water near the beaver dam and outlet of the lake. This usually means that some larger fish are cruising for a meal, but we did not see any fish or rises. For all of our effort, there were no hits.

Doug continually wore his old baseball cap when he was outside, and John did likewise when he was fishing. My old Indiana Jones-style fishing hat seemed to fascinate Doug. Over the two days we were there, I added various flies to my hatband. After using each of these flies, I put them on my hatband to dry out. I also added a grouse feather Doug had given me. As we were leaving the lodge, I watched him admiring my hat. It became customized to the local area.

We came back to the lodge and finished packing for the trip home. I took the opportunity for one last shower so that I would feel clean for the rest of the trip home. John and I checked out with Marge, and Doug drove us to the Témmisami train station, all of three minutes away.

By this time, we were seasoned train travelers. We did not expect the train to be on time. We bought food at the only grocery food store in town, which is a co-op. We bought enough to eat and drink for lunch and dinner for about $10CDN. This saved us a lot of money compared to the prices on the train.

The southbound train was 50 minutes late. It was about 1½ hours late by the time we pulled in to Toronto's Union Station. John talked to the conductor, who said that he had been working on this line for three years and it has not been on time yet. Although the train did not pull in until almost 9:00PM, we decided to drive until we got home.

John was a good driver and we both called our wives on the way home to assure them that we were okay. The only excitement was that we were stopped at the border crossing. Our car tested positive for radiation. A recorded voice in the immigration control booth kept repeating "ALERT, ALERT, and ALERT." We could hear it in the car. I wondered if they were going to let us back in the country!

The Homeland Security person at the booth asked if either of us recently had a medical procedure done. I said, "Yes." Fortunately, the hospital had given me a card saying what the procedure was. They took our identification and my card and directed us to an inspection bay. I had to explain to the border patrol officers that I had a nuclear medicine procedure done several weeks before. I was injected with a radioactive isotope of gadolinium, Ga-67. The level of radiation in my body by now must be very low. However, my presence in the van was enough to trigger an alert. I was told to get out of the car and they had John drive the car through a radiation detector. It read nothing. They used some portable scanner on me and it identified Ga-67 as the isotope.

They apologized for the inconvenience but said that they had to have the alarms trigger on very low levels, because someone trying to smuggle something radioactive into the country would have it heavily shielded. The Homeland Security guards said that an alert due to medical procedures happens about 25 times a day. After checking us out, they gave us back our identification, and let us go. I actually thanked them for doing their job so thoroughly.

All I can say is, "Wow, what an experience!" This was something I never expected on this trip. I thought that all our adventures were over. I can just image what our city's major morning newspaper would have said in their front-page article, "Two local men arrested at the Canadian border by Homeland Security for conspiracy to smuggle radioactive substance into the country." "Black proclaims innocence." Black told investigators, "We were fishing. He asked me to drive. I didn't know he was radioactive." Prosecutors are suspicious of their cover story. Inside sources allege, "They had fishing equipment with them. They went to Canada, but didn't actually catch any fish."

We stopped once for gas and fast food. When I went to pay, I had to stop and think, because I had Canadian currency and coins mixed with U.S. money. This seemed very normal the entire time we were in Canada, but now in the U.S., it seemed strange. How quickly we adjust to local conditions or customs. We arrived home at 2:30AM in the morning. It took us 14 hours to go 600 miles. This trip had everything but fish.

I called Doug on Saturday, and told him we arrived safely home last night. He told me that it rained all day. Only three fish were caught, two pickerel and one walleye for 15 people fishing from his lodge. Not good. No one knows why the fish aren't hitting yet. I told him that we accidentally stole the blue ice from the freezer in our apartment. My wife found it when we unpacked the soft-sided cooler this morning. I told him that I would send it to him. He said, no, that people leave them there all the time and that they have plenty of them. He said that they would have never known if I hadn't told them.

I went back to work on Monday. At noon, I went to Half-Price Books near my office at lunchtime and bought some religious books. I selected what I though was a large variety. I added some books from my own bookshelf to fill the box to the top. I sent some recipes, including those for scones and shortbread, to Marge and this large box of pastoral literature.

I called Doug the following Wednesday. He said that it snowed since we were there and was snowing again that day. Furthermore, he reported that only a dozen fish were caught since we were there and only six of them were keepers. I do not know if he was just feeding me a fish tale so that I would feel better about our lack of luck or not, but the details made the story feel true.

"Bill," Doug said in conclusion, "I'm sorry, but some days even the guide can't catch a fish. Look, if you want to come up next year at this time, I will spend some time this summer locating trout." I asked him to do that. If Doug can actually locate some trout in the region, I hope to return someday.

It occurred to me that I should ask the Lake Airways where the trout are. I called Lake Airways and talked to Darren, the bush pilot. He said that there are trout in Turner Lake, approximately 21 miles away, and Trethewey Lake, approximately 48 miles away. The cost of a round trip to Turner is $600 and to Trethewey is $1,200. I plotted these locations on my GPS maps, but the prices seemed too steep for my vacation budget. Later I discovered that a road passes near Turner Lake which would only require a 0.2 mile hike the final leg, but Trethewey Lake would be a 2½ drive with more than a one mile hike carrying a canoe and all our supplies.

John's and my homes are at 41 degrees north latitude and the Northland Lodge is at 47 degrees north latitude, a difference of almost exactly 400 north-south miles, not to mention an even bigger difference in attitude and lifestyle. After reflecting on the trip as a whole, and with the perspective of the passing of time, I still wonder whether the whole thing was a wild "Canadian" goose chase, or whether through some divine providence, we were meant to be there. I will probably never know for sure. But whether chance or fate, I hope that Marge enjoys her "new" books, I certainly enjoyed the journey and the adventure, and John told me that he did, too, even though we did not catch any fish.

Epilogue

After I essentially completed the above story and exactly 12 days after John and I left, I got a call from a very excited, joyous and bubbly Marge.

"Hi," she said, "today is my birthday. I got the box with the books in it." The only logical connection I could think of for her mentioning this is that she felt the box of books was some kind of birthday present. I did not even know when her birthday was.

"Hi, Marge," I said in return, but got no further than that.

"You were sent to us. You were sent to us," she kept saying over and over again. She then proceeded to catch her breath and explained that one of the books I had put in the box was about conducting all kinds of worship services. I remembered trying to put in the box a variety of religious books that I thought may be of use to her, and did not consider any one of them more important than the others.

Marge said that her church had been praying on how to get the children more involved in worship services. They knew that God wanted them to do this, but did not know exactly what to do. The worship service book had an entire chapter that laid out in detail how to accomplish this. She was very grateful, and said that as far as she and her congregation were concerned, God had personally sent John and me as the answer to their prayers.

As I started to comprehend the full implications of what she was saying, all of the hairs on the back of my neck stood up. Was this entire adventure an extremely long and improbable string of coincidences, or did John and I just witness, and even unknowingly participate in, God intervening in human affairs? I cannot imagine that I was selected to go to there because I am anyone special, and cannot see why I was selected for this job. I do not think that I had any special qualifications other than an ordinary belief in Christianity. I wondered whether I had free will or was guided to be at that exact place at that exact time.

At first, I thought that this was a simple fishing story. Maybe it still is, although not in the way that I first thought.

Afterword

The Ontario Northlander Train route (passenger) has been discontinued since this expedition. It has been replaced with a bus service. When I found out, I was sad for days at this loss of an adventure experience for future fishermen and other travelers.

The Trouble With Scottish Flies

In the summer of 2008, on short notice, I found myself going to London, England, for a few days on business. I had not been to England for several years, and actually thought that I would visit Scotland before I visited England again. My wife and I had been planning a summer vacation to Scotland each year for about three years, but something always came up causing us to defer this trip. Mostly it was the lack of time, an illness or other family commitments.

As we were planning this trip, we wanted to accomplish several things: See the Scottish countryside, learn about one of my wife's ancestors, Sir William Hardie of Edinburgh, visit a shortbread factory, visit a single-malt whiskey distillery, and of course, fly fish on some famous river. As anyone who has ever been married can attest, joint vacation planning with a spouse who does not fish involves compromises, and should be considered completely different from planning a fishing trip with your friends. It should be obvious which destinations were hers and which were mine, although I will admit under duress to partial ownership of the shortbread stop.

Normally, when on a business trip, regardless of city or country, I try to visit a local fly shop to purchase a few flies. I always ask to talk to the shop's fishing manager or expert.

"Where can I go around here to catch fish?" is usually my first question. "What flies work on these streams?" is the second.

Sometimes I need to ask these questions in another language. Prior to traveling to a country where English is not the primary tongue, I always learn a few fly fishing words in that other language. I have never failed to communicate, although from time to time I have had to pantomime some phrases or actions. For example, holding your hands apart, palms facing inward is the universal symbol for the size of the fish you caught. This is usually greeted with mirth and skepticism, regardless of what country the shop is located in.

I always purchase one each of the recommended flies, take them home and reverse engineer them. I tie about a dozen of each kind and bring them on the next trip to that locale when I intend to do some fly fishing.

On this trip, I wanted to find a fly shop in London that could provide useful advice about flies in Scotland. I looked on the internet, and discovered an Orvis store on Dover Street in London. This was close to my hotel and coincidentally quite near Buckingham Palace.

"How can I not go?" I asked myself, knowing the answer in advance.

During my first day in London, I made time to visit that Orvis store. I travelled in a traditional black London taxicab with my local host, Tom Tibbs. The streets were crowded with cars, buses, trucks and pedestrians, but our driver was skillful, getting us to our destination in record time. I was glad someone else drove, realizing that my instincts were all wrong for driving on the left side of the road. Tom and I stepped out of the taxi and went up a short flight of stairs to the store. Inside, the store looked like any Orvis store in the United States with the same color scheme, merchandise format, products, and displays.

"What flies will work for trout in Scotland?" I asked the store's fishing manager.

After some discussion, he gave me one each of the following: Invicta, Silver Butcher, March Brown, Teal Blue and Silver, and a Silver March Brown. He sold me these flies in a small multi-compartment plastic box, which had printed on it, "Orvis, 36a Dover Street, London." I immediately realized that this box would make a nice keepsake.
"That will be £3 30 pence for the entire lot, including the box," said the fishing manager. Automatically, I converted this amount in my head to about $5.00 US dollars.
"Not a bad price," I thought as I paid the bill.
"Are there any special instructions on how to successfully fish these flies?" I asked.
"You must fish these flies wet," he replied. "These flies will work well on Speyside rivers," he concluded with confidence.

As we were leaving the store, Tom pointed to a book that was being prominently displayed and promoted entitled, A Green Life by Clare Dickson.

"Look at this," Tom said with pride. He opened one of the books on display and showed me that it was dedicated to him.

"How is this possible?" I asked Tom in astonishment. The book was about an environmentally friendly lifestyle in the United Kingdom, and Tom was a physicist with a PhD from Imperial College in advanced semiconductors.

"I am a technical consultant and spokesman for the Green Movement here in the United Kingdom," said Tom. "The author and my mother are best friends. Clarissa lives in Scotland, just outside of Edinburgh."

When the sales manager heard us talking, she said that all of the Orvis stores in the U.K. were currently promoting this book.

"Do you think the author would be willing to come to our Edinburgh store and sign autographs?" she asked.

"Please give me the contact information of your sales manager in the Edinburgh store," said Tom. "I will make sure that the author gets this message. Whether she responds or not, is of course, up to her."

We left the store, and walked to end of Dover Street to Piccadilly to catch a cab. At the corner, I could see Green Park and Buckingham Palace directly across the road. Only then did I put together the conjecture that Balmoral Castle was on the "Speyside" of Scotland, just west of Aberdeen. It is well known that the Royals fly fish when they are there. I never thought to ask while in the store, but suddenly I wondered where they bought their flies? This fly shop was certainly close enough. Of course, the store would go to them, not the other way around. It brought a smile to imagine that I may have visited the "Royal" Orvis store, although there was no sign outside that said, "By appointment to His Majesty."

When I arrived back home in Cleveland, I looked through my library of fly-fishing books, and after a few minutes found all the patterns for the flies I had bought. I then went through my inventory of materials, located what I had in stock, and made a list of what I needed. A week later, I went to the state capitol on business and visited an Orvis dealer, where I picked up almost all of the missing materials. The two things they did not have were, a hen pheasant wing and tail and a blue jay feather.

The hen pheasant feather is required for the March Brown, Silver March Brown and Invicta.

Brian, the storeowner, promised to order the hen pheasant wing and tail. This store carries male pheasant feathers, as does every other fly shop and catalog store in the U.S. They do not carry the hen feather because there is no demand for it. After two weeks, they called me to explain that they could not order it, either, because it is imported and quarantined because of the fear of spreading bird flu.

The blue jay feather is required for the Invicta, but I was confident that I could get this by other means. I told my fishing buddy Rodger about my need for a blue jay feather.

"No problem," he said. "I have a pellet gun and they are a real backyard nuisance." I looked at many other sources for hen pheasant skins, calling all the usual well-known distributors, and searching the internet without any luck. I also contacted a fly shop in New Brunswick, Canada, which is across the St. Johns River from Fort Kent, Maine. The owner said he would look for a hen pheasant skin and get back to me with the cost. He said he mails all his products for his U.S. customers from the Fort Kent post office. He said this avoids delays and higher mailing costs, and I am thinking probably customs inspections, too. I am not sure whether this is strictly legal or not but it probably makes the shop much more profitable. He never did get back to me.

I even contacted Tom Tibbs for his assistance in getting a hen pheasant skin. He said his brother was a hunter and that he would talk to him. Tom later told me that his brother couldn't help.

Finally, I saw an advertisement in an Orvis newsletter for one of their resorts located in Pennsylvania. They are an Orvis-endorsed lodge that provides fly-fishing and hunting trips (including pheasant and grouse). I called them and talked to Dave, their 'trap and hunt' staff member. He emailed me and said that he would save me a hen pheasant skin from the next hunt scheduled for two weekends hence. We exchanged emails and agreed to keep in touch. He told me he is a fly fisherman and fly tier, too. I sent him a copy of my recipe for the Pine Creek Sparkle Nymph, one of my favorite and most productive flies, to thank him in advance for his help.

Not willing to wait any longer, I tied the Teal Blue and Silver, and then the Silver Butcher while I waited for the hen pheasant feathers to show up.

Finally, Dave emailed me in December of 2008 saying that they bagged some hen pheasants in their last hunt. He said he would skin one and salt it for a few days to cure it and then mail it to me. Dave cured the skin in salt and hung it up to dry in the equipment shed where they store their all-terrain vehicles. Somehow, a feral cat got into the shed and tore the skin to shreds. I had to wait until February of 2009, when Dave bagged another hen pheasant. This time he made sure that no cat could get at the skin.

The skin finally arrived in the mail from Dave. In eager anticipation, I opened the bag and examined the feathers. I noted that the skin was still wet in some spots. Worried that it would rot, I immediately called Dave and explained the situation.

"What do I do?" I asked him.

"I wouldn't leave it in the bag for now," was his reply. "It needs to dry a little more and the salt helps with the process. What I generally do is put salt on the meaty areas, let it sit, dust it off, and if still looks moist keep repeating until the moisture is gone. This is similar to salt curing meat. The salt acts as a preservative. Once all the moisture is out, the skin will last forever. I have rabbit, squirrel, coyote, deer, and all kinds of skins I have done this way. Good luck."

So I covered the wet spots with salt and left them to dry in my basement. Now my wife is a saint and very tolerant of my fly-fishing and tying activities, but I felt I had to at least warn her.

"Oh, Dear," I said, in what I thought was my most pleasant tone of voice. "Please don't be upset when you walk by my fly-tying bench and see a fresh pheasant skin lying there all covered in salt. This is entirely normal." Her only response was to shake her head and give me a disgusted look our family calls "the hairy eyeball."

I also posed the question of curing bird skin to Doug Adams. He and his wife Marge own and run a fishing lodge in Temmaga, Ontario, located about 300 miles north of Toronto. He is also a fishing guide and fur trapper. I spent a few days fishing at his lodge a year ago and got to know him and his wife.

"Good question," he said. "I'd suggest removing all the fat and meat that you can possibly get off and then 'wash' the whole thing in a bath of the white gas, Coleman fuel, or naphtha that you'd use in outdoor lanterns and those old two-burner stoves. This will remove any grease left on the skin as well as any oils remaining on the feathers. Put it in a pail or plastic container, making sure to wear rubber gloves to keep the liquid off your hands, and swish it around for a couple minutes. Do not ring it out or whip it around but let the liquid drip off for a few seconds then put it in a large paper bag that has some powdered plaster of Paris in it. Shake or tumble it around (with the top of the bag securely closed) to mix the powder through it.

"Although the hide will appear 'wet,' it will not dissolve in the powder to make mud. The powder will absorb any remaining naphtha fuel and soften the hide. It only takes a minute or two to do the trick. Remove it and shake out any remaining powder. A vacuum sweeper on reverse (blow, not suck) will remove the last remnants of the powder. You are finished. It will probably stiffen up, but you can drape the hide over something to attain your preferred shape before it dries too hard, probably in a half hour or so. This is how a taxidermist preserves bird skins to be mounted. Trust me, it works.

"One more thing. Your wife will appreciate you doing all of this outside.... especially the part where you blow the powder out of the hide after you tan it. For the next one you get, forget the part about salting it down before tanning it. Hope to see you next summer. Oh yes, Marge says to say hello."

After hearing this, I decided that I would continue with the salt process this time as the easiest course of action. Maybe next time I get a skin I will go the naphtha route. I actually located a gallon at work that could work, just in case.

I had been unable to locate a source of blue jay feathers in the U.S. and my friend Rodger never actually shot at a blue jay, much less hit one. About this time I began to realize that blue jays must fall in the 'songbird' category, and because of this, it is illegal to hunt blue jays in the U.S., or even possess their feathers. Naturally, this would make the blue jay feather difficult to acquire as well.

Then in March of 2009, I had the opportunity to go to London again for work. I called the "royal" Orvis store and inquired about blue jay feathers, only to learn that they did not carry them. Then I called Venard, a venerable distributor of feathers and other fly-tying materials in the United Kingdom.

"Does your firm carry blue jay feathers?" I asked their sales manager over the phone.

"Yes," he replied.

"Great," I said. "I am in London. Do you have any nearby outlets?"

"Yes, Farrow's on Pall Mall and Granger's in South Kensington," he responded. "They are both retail shops."

I looked up the location of each fly shop on a London Underground map and determined that Granger's was close to a stop on the Underground District Line. As I was using public transportation this trip, it was convenient to try Granger's first. They had everything I needed. I purchased additional mallard blues (Butcher Blues) for the Silver Butcher, although I already had some, and several packages of "jay" feathers for the Invicta. The packaging did not say "blue jay" but rather "European Jay." I think that this is their way of avoiding any legal problems.

I also purchased one each: Gray Duster, Quill Ginger, and March Brown dry flies to reverse engineer. The Donega Company in Ireland tied these flies. Granger's proprietor said that these would also work well in Scotland. These flies were beautiful. Their most prominent characteristic was the ingenious use of cul de canard feathers (CDC puffs) in their construction.

As I was packing for my return to the U.S., I was worried that I could not bring the feathers I had purchased into this country. However, since they were commercially packaged, and did not say "blue jay'" customs did not object.

After reverse engineering these flies and determining their materials and tying techniques, I purchased some CDC puffs in the correct colors to make these flies. I quickly tied up a batch of each. When finished, I told my wife that I was ready to go to Scotland.

"Let's see," said my wife. "Two trips to London, one trip to the state capitol, covering a bird skin in salt for months in our basement, and innumerable hours plotting and scheming to find the right materials, not to mention the hour or two that it actually took you to do the tying."

"After all this trouble, wouldn't it have been easier to just buy the flies?" asked my wife.

"Yes," I responded. "But not nearly as much fun."

Afterword

Many outfitters have since begun carrying hen pheasant skins, maybe because of my several calls to them, or probably because the ban has been lifted. In addition, several outfitters in the U.S. now carry "European Jay Wings."

Joining a Fishing Federation Club

In 2009 I joined a local affiliate of the Federation of Fishermen. I attended my first meeting in early March. This meeting was billed as the annual fly-tying marathon. I emailed the president of the club stating that I was a fly tier and asking if I should bring anything. The answer was "definitely yes. Bring all your tying gear and some patterns." So I packed up my vice, light, magnifier, tools, materials and journal. I also made up a few copies of my favorite fly recipe and a large copy of a list of my fly patterns. I brought a representative selection of the flies I had tied.

This particular meeting was held at one of the county Metroparks. I walked in with my paraphernalia, signed the roster and was given one raffle ticket. I paid my dues and purchased a club pin. I set up the items I brought on an eight-foot folding table. There were 20 such tables; all were occupied. In addition, there were two tables pushed together for a teacher and six students who were learning to tie a wooly bugger, one of the easiest and most basic flies to for a beginner to tie. Only about 20 visitors showed up all evening to view the 'wares' of the fly tiers.

After arranging my display, I made a point of walking around, looking critically at each tier's table, and talking to each tier. I put the club pin on my sweater so that they would know that I belonged to their organization. They all apparently knew each other and recognized that I was a new member.

"Are you new?" some of them even asked.
"Yes," I always responded with a big smile and an outstretched hand. I introduced myself and asked questions about their flies and tying.

One of the first things I recognized was that the vices of the other participants were much, much more expensive than mine. For the first nine years that I tied flies, my bench vice was a thin diameter post with a 'C' clamp on one end, and miniature jaws on the other. The jaws used an

'O' ring for compression to hold the hook. It cost about $45. About one year ago, I moved up to a well-known travel vice at a cost of about $165. This vice had a "C" clamp on one end, but on the other a rotary clamping mechanism, much superior to the "O" ring technology. I was astounded that the other participants had vices that cost from $345 up to $695. I knew these prices well because I had shopped around before I bought the one I was using. I had the least expensive vice in the entire group! I could not believe the amount of money that was spent on vices.

Most of the others had display cases for their flies. It never occurred to me to have a display case. My flies were still in their plastic boxes where I stored them after making them. The box bins are all labeled as to the name of the fly and size of the hook. No one else did this. My boxes are functional, not decorative. I take flies out of these boxes to go fishing. I wish this was completely true, but alas it is not, as I end up giving away more than half the flies I tie.

I noticed that most of the others only tie a few patterns. I tie almost 100. Some had a few, some had more than several dozen, but none were as varied as mine. Not only that, but many of the tiers were not interested in learning new patterns. This was one of the main reasons I come to these events, to learn new things. They were not interested in receiving a copy of my nymph tying instructions, even when I handed them one.

I quickly realized that only one tier at the meeting was a much better tier that I was. He had on display patterns he created that had been published in national magazines. He had these magazines open to his patterns. I was impressed. But he only ties a few different patterns; he just varies the colors. I looked at his display of nearly four dozen flies for a few moments and it occurred to me what he had done.

"You only have two basic patterns here, the rest are just color variations," I said to him.
"You are right," he said in astonishment, as he looked up at me with a smile on his face. Apparently, no one else had noticed his strategy.

"It's all right," I said. "I do the same thing on some steelhead patterns I learned from a local fishing guide." After some small talk and admiring his display for a while, I spied what I thought was his best pattern.

"Can I have a copy of that pattern to reverse engineer?" I said pointing to what I thought was his best pattern. "Is it productive for trout?"

"You bet," he said, giving one to me. By the expression on his face, you would have thought that I had just given him a present. I looked at the fly closely and told him what materials he used to make it.

"Am I right?" I asked to confirm my guesses.

"You're right," he exclaimed, astonished for the second time, at my ability to do this.

"How could these guys tie flies and yet be so ignorant of common materials?" I thought. I invited him to come over and look at my fly patterns.

He and I were the only participants that tied flies to target specific streams, seasons, and locations. Why else would I tie them? What were the motives of the other participants? Maybe they do not fish far from home and this is not an issue for them.

After the show, a short business meeting was held. Only about a dozen people stayed. After the meeting the president announced the drawing for the door prizes. There were about eight of them. Some were pretty nice. I pulled out the one blue ticket I was given and looked at the number. I looked to my left and my right and noticed that each of the other members had about three dozen blue tickets each. I laughed out loud. The person who signed me in only gave me one. Could it be possible that this drawing was rigged to favor the good 'ole boys?

Obviously, my chances of winning anything were close to zero. I didn't win anything, and during the drawing I wondered how long I had to attend these meetings to be considered one of the good 'ole boys and get three dozen raffle tickets, too.

I learned many things at this meeting. Among them, I was not such a bad fly tier, my bench vice is inexpensive compared to others, I made more and different patterns – targeted to specific situations than anyone else there, and I didn't have any fly display capability. I was much more eager to learn new patterns than any of the experienced tiers there.

After the meeting I emailed the president of the club asking for the contact information for Andy, the tier whose flies I admired, sure that he was the person I want to learn from. The president of the club sent me his email address. In my first email to him, I told him that I had indeed reverse engineered his fly pattern and loved its simplicity and beauty. Furthermore, I had named it the "Settlers' Special" His response to my original email was as follows:

"Received your e-mail and appreciate you considering me as a good fly tier. I always felt I was at least above average. I am glad you gave my fly a name, now I don't have to. I started to keep a log of my flies but got lazy and stopped. I tie many of my flies that are common to the streams in my home state. I tie a lot from "take-offs." I see a nice pattern of some kind and tie it a different way with other materials and they really come out good. The best thing is that most of them work."

I told him that I considered him the best tier there including me. I asked, "Where exactly are you from and where do you fish?" He answered me. I told him where I fished and that I was born there. I sent him a list of flies I tie.

"You have quite a collection of flies. A lot of good ones," he responded. "I started to keep a record of the flies I tied, but stopped. I was tying all kinds and every type you could think of. I tied a lot of the same patterns you tied and many steelhead patterns. I promise this year I will make a list and send it to you or see you and give it to you. The trouble is, I tied many nice and good patterns but never attached names. I once went to Oak Orchard Creek with a friend and never had a strike with what they said was good to use. I put on one of my homemade "no name" special and caught three "steelies" and one nice brown. That's what I meant by not keeping record and list."

"As for me, I came from a little town called Kent and went to high school in the town of Indiana. Yes, I fished the same river you did and lived on locks 7, 8, and 9, and every place in between that you could name. I fished all the streams you fished and many more."

I thanked him for his response and asked, "Are you planning to go to the next Federation meeting? If so, maybe we can meet for dinner somewhere close before the meeting. My treat!

"Furthermore, it is a small world. I know where Kent is! My wife and I are from small towns not too far from Kent. I have been through Kent many times. My aunt and uncle lived in Indiana." I told him their names. "He worked in the coalmines. She worked in a doctor's office. She was from Plumville. I spent many days as a youth at their house."

"Yes, it's a small world," Andy responded. "They were the best of friends with my wife's uncle and aunt. They were also at our wedding. How about them apples?"

Before the next club meeting, I arranged to meet him and his wife for dinner at a nearby restaurant. At dinner, she told me that my uncle and her uncle, and two others were all foremen in the mines and very good friends. They and their wives were very close. They all took turns visiting each other's houses. People socialized this way during that era in rural areas. The men played poker a lot. My uncle had a fancy poker table in his finished basement. He also had a reprint of one of the 16 Dogs Playing Poker oil paintings by C.M. Coolidge, titled A Friend in Need, commissioned in 1903 by Brown & Bigelow to advertise cigars. This large print hung on a wall over the poker table.

The men all played on the mine's ball team. My uncle was left handed and played part of one season as a first baseman on a professional baseball league team when he was about 21, so this fits facts we already know. Andy's wife said that my uncle did not like the curfews and other restrictions on his social life that the ball team imposed, so he quit playing professional baseball. The couples danced at the Elks. His wife remembered that my aunt made peach preserves and plum jam. This fits with my childhood memories, too. She always had delicious homemade jam on the table when we visited.

The first part of the fishing meeting featured a noted fly tier demonstrating how to tie his favorite fly. I immediately went over to see the demonstration. The tier was surrounded by about six others and tying something out of the Dave Hughes book Essential Flies. I was so disappointed. I have that book. There was nothing new to learn from him on this night.

One of the unexpected benefits of hosting my new friend and his wife for dinner was that he proceeded to introduce me to practically everyone in the club. They all knew him, and by extension, I was cordially welcomed. This was a far different reception than the first meeting. Andy showed his friends my fishing journal and stories. They were all impressed with my organization, level of detail, and how I illustrated tying in my files.

Andy has a cabin, named Hunters Sunrise, very near Tinkersville and close to Oak Creek. I showed him my GPS maps and fishing spots of that area. He knew all of them and suggested that we also fish four others. He located each place on my GPS map. He invited me to visit him at his cabin whenever he is there and I am in the area. Andy knew of the Tinkersville Hardware, and the Arcadian Restaurant.

The main speaker at this meeting was George Vossily. He talked about fishing in Saskatchewan for northern pike on a fly. He caught many pike from 40 to 50 inches long. He says that he used a 9-weight rod with 1/0 to 3/0 hooks (Mustad 3407 saltwater), a steel leader, and a figure 8 knot. He said his most productive flies, in order (best–first) were: black Dahlberg diver, chartreuse over white Clouser minnow, Orange Surprise, green Lefty's Deceiver, and Red/White soft hackle. He said we should all learn how to do a double haul cast to shoot our lines out 100 feet.

His presentation was a digital slide show. In addition, he had videos of catching pike and fly tying embedded in the show. His fly tying videographer was there and said that the video camera was positioned about 6-8 inches from the vice. He said that the video editing program is equally as important as the camera.

After this extended welcome, I am pleased to be a member of such a quality Federation Club. The friendliness and quality of the people make the club!

Connaught Creek Trip

In early May, I called Great River Tackle to ask about water conditions, fishing reports, and for recommendations on good fishing spots for the upcoming weekend.

"The river is too muddy to fish, but Connaught Creek clears before the river, and it should be clear enough to fish well by this weekend" said the store owner. "Assuming we don't have any more major rain storms," he added. So my friend Rodger, my daughter, and I decided to go to Connaught Creek to fish for steelhead.

I have a fly-fishing map that covers this area entitled, "3-C-U Trout Association Connaught Creek Fisherman's Map and Access Guide" and used it to plan the trip. I had been to Connaught Creek several times over the last 10 years and had notated the map as to where I had gone on each of those trips. My intentions were for us to hit two spots on the creek with a meal between at a local diner.

Early that Saturday morning Rodger drove to my house, arriving about 6:00AM. Together we left in my Jeep to pick up my daughter at a restaurant just east of an interstate highway split. Our fishing party complete, we then travelled east on the interstate to an exit about 35 miles away, all nice interstate roads so far.

After we got off the interstate, we drove on secondary roads to our first fishing spot, the State Street covered bridge access site. The last few miles are gravel roads. Near our destination, we saw a flock of turkeys crossing the road. I stopped my Jeep and waited for them to cross. Not only did we see them, but we could hear them too. They were very noisy and were fun to listen to. The covered bridge we were going to was built in 1983. I believe that the purpose of modern covered bridges is to help Amish horses avoid slipping on the ice and hurting themselves during the winter. This presupposes Amish live in the area. Sure enough, we saw an

Amish man and a boy in a horse drawn wagon with a rowboat in it during this trip. We waved.

We parked my Jeep on a muddy area just off the road, put on our waders, and strung up our rods. A funny-looking male duck stood in the parking area. He did not appear to be overly afraid of us nor would he move away. We kept an eye on him, and he on us. We speculated that he was from a local farm. There were many farms in the area.

My daughter was planning to use the bamboo rod that I had restored for her for the very first time and I was going to use my high-end Orvis graphite rod for the very first time. I also gave my daughter my mid-arbor reel to use with her rod.

"Wow!" said Rodger as he noticed the rod tube that my rod came in, laying in the back of the Jeep. The color of the tube is dark green but in sunlight, it looks like a hologram with a golden weave deep below the surface. I put the rod together and handed it to him without saying anything. He waved the rod, as if he were casting, and then carefully studied the rod itself for a moment.

"This looks like a really high-end rod" he said.

"Yep," I responded, "I got it for Christmas."

We put on our waders and fishing vests, and strung up our rods. After we finished getting ready, we crossed over the bridge, and walked downstream less than a ¼ mile. All of us started fishing for steelhead, using some light colored streamers I had tied. Light colors flies work best when the water is clear. Dark color flies work best when the water is muddy. This water was not gin clear but it certainly was not muddy. The person I talked to at Grand River Tackle was right about the stream conditions. The bottom was visible. I also noticed that the flow rate was much higher than it usually is in the summer.

I slowly moved downstream after covering a particular stretch of water. I usually take two steps and then repeat my casting pattern. As I was fishing, trying to cover as much water as I could, I snagged my fly in a tree behind me. I was paying more attention to the stream than to the possibility that I had no room behind me for the backcast. I reached up to the lowest branch and pulled it down toward me. This was early spring and the leaves were only buds. This enabled me to see the bare branches. As I reached for my fly, I found two other flies in the same branch that appeared to be left there from last fishing season. Laughing to myself, I removed them.

"Look at this" I said to Rodger and my daughter later, as I showed them the two flies and explained how I got them. "I am not the only one who has tree trouble."

After a while, with no hits on my streamer for steelhead, I switched to a #12 "Joe Humphries" style sulfur nymph pattern (brown and yellow) that I had recently tied, and started fishing for trout. Looking around, I noticed that my daughter was having trouble with her rod. I was concerned about this, as I felt responsible for the quality of the rod. Upon close inspection, I saw that she inadvertently put the line through the keeper ring and this was impeding easy line control.

"Here," I said, handing her my rod. "Let me fix your rod for you. It will just take a moment, and will make fishing so much easier for you." She took mine and handed me hers, I sat down on a rock and started rethreading her fly line. After a few minutes, I heard her call me. She was standing not very far away.

"Dad, Dad, oh Dad!" she said. I looked up and saw my daughter holding an 8-inch rainbow trout. She had caught it on my equipment using a fly I had tied. I was glad she had caught it, but could not help thinking that I should have been the one to catch that fish! After a few moments, we slipped the fish off the hook and it swam away.

We watched three deer cross the creek not far from us. There were deer tracks and raccoon tracks all over the sandy areas near the creek. Neither Rodger nor I caught anything in that area, and after a while, we decided to leave for lunch. For future reference, I measured and recorded the following weather information: water temperature 54°F, air temperature 62°F, sunshine and high cirrus clouds, and little to no wind.

We drove to the Main Street Diner in Connaught, Ohio, where they advertise breakfast all day. The diner was originally a railroad car with several additions. The outside is painted an awful shade of blue. Inside there is a long row of stools in front of a counter and some tables. The diner had old-fashioned décor. This was not an affectation. It looked like it had seen better days.

The diner was about three-quarters full and somehow these patrons seemed to fit right in. They looked fairly scruffy, too. We had no room to complain; we went in still wearing our waders. We sat down at a nearby table. The place mats were paper and contained advertisements around the edges for local businesses. You don't see much of that anymore.

We each ordered a different breakfast. Rodger had a ham and cheese omelet with toast and my daughter had over-easy eggs, toast and corned beef hash. I had ordinary French toast with syrup. Before eating, I went to the restroom to wash my hands. The first step onto the ceramic floor in the men's washroom practically caused me to do a split. I forgot that I was wearing wading shoes with carbide studs. With no traction, as soon as I put my weight on it, my foot started sliding across the smooth floor at a high rate of speed. I caught myself just in time on a sink, avoiding what I am sure would have been a very painful injury that would have cut our fishing trip short.

At lunch, my daughter, Rodger and I talked about many contemporary issues such as business, politics and her impending job loss in the marketing department at City Bank.

"Do you realize," she said, "that I am paying taxes to the federal government to provide TARP money for a Pittsburgh bank to buy City Bank, which will lay me off as soon as the acquisition is completed." This succinct analysis really impressed me.

We cleaned our plates and drained our cups before heading off to our next fishing spot. The access point to this fishing spot is the Keefer Road Bridge over Connaught Creek. The notation on my map said to fish the downstream side. This location was only a few miles outside of town and it took us only minutes to get there. I had never fished this exact spot, but I had fished this area from another access road farther downstream, and coincidentally closer to town. When we pulled into the parking area, we noticed a Jeep with New York license plates and a "Buffalo" license plate holder.

We quickly strung up our rods and headed to the stream. Immediately, we saw two men about 50 yards downstream. Only one had a rod and the other kept pointing across the stream at a specific location. After a few minutes, we realized that we were watching a guide and his client working the creek.

We stood there in amazement as we watched the client pull four large steelhead out of the stream, one right after another in the space of ½ hour. Meanwhile, the three of us were getting no hits at all, only a couple dozen yards away. The client appeared to have a combination nymph, weight, and floating strike indicator on his line (in that order). It looked like the guide had tied this on for him.

My daughter had the most nerve. As they were leaving that spot, she walked over to the guide.

"Say, I just saw you guys pull four steelhead out of that spot," she said. "If you don't mind me asking, what kind of fly are you using?"

"Here, I'll show you," said the guide, giving her two flies. "These flies are meant to resemble bleeding minnows." The flies were white with a hint of red in them. They resembled wooly buggers but had some red color and some flash in them. I then walked over to her and the guide, and he gave me five more flies, all different patterns.

"All of these flies will catch fish in this creek," he stated with absolute assurance. "I took 15 steelhead out of a spot just above the bridge three days ago." Based upon the performance we both just witnessed, we believed him!

"Thank you very much," we both said.

He said he was from Buffalo and we told him where we were from. He did not introduce himself.

"What's your name?" I asked as he was walking away. "Mike Prairie" he answered.

We watched Mike and his client walk downstream to fish a different spot. By now, it was our time to leave for the day. However, before we left, I stood high on the creek bank near where Mike's client caught so many fish, and studied the exact spot where the client was casting. I quickly realized that I would have walked by this spot 100 times without noticing anything special about it. I certainly never would have concluded a steelhead would hide there.

But after studying the water for a few minutes, I noticed that Mike and his client must have been standing high on a pile of underwater rocks in the creek. This would allow for improved vision and a better casting angle. There was a single line of riffles across the stream on the water above this spot, indicating a drop off. This white water would provide some additional oxygen in the water and the drop off would provide deeper water for the steelhead to lie in. On the far side, the stream flowed swiftly through a channel.

Behind the fast water, next to the shore was an eddy, back flowing against current. This was creating a pocket of absolutely still water right next to the swift current. This transition of current speeds is known as a seam. Mike was pointing at it and must have been telling the client to cast the fly to that seam or to the pocket. Fish would not have to use much energy to remain stationary and could dart out into the swift current to eat any food that the current would bring to them, sort of like the "dim sum" cart coming to your table in a Chinese restaurant! With all these piscatorial advantages, it certainly made a great place for large fish to "hold" there in the stream.

We climbed the bank back to the parking lot and took off our waders and fishing vests. I know it was a coincidence but my daughter and Rodger both had leaky waders – I need to remember to patch her inside right leg at the seam, where the black boot meets the green fabric.

I did not catch a fish on this trip, but felt that the entire trip was worth it. I had the opportunity to try out my new graphite rod. It was very light and the action was wonderful. My daughter was able to try out her bamboo rod. She loved the action of her rod and by the end of the trip, she was casting her flies much farther than she ever could before. It amazes me that 90-year-old bamboo still beats the best high bulk modulus graphite (or boron) composites that modern technology can provide. Mother Nature is still ahead in this area. My daughter also liked my mid-arbor reel.

I felt that I had gained a lot of knowledge on this trip. I now know a hot spot or two in this creek. I also have a better idea of what to look for in reading water for likely places for steelhead to hide. In addition, I now have 5-6 steelhead fly patterns that will work on this creek, created by an expert who knows how to catch steelhead. I plan on reverse engineering these patterns and tying some to use when I come back again. I hope that this will be sooner rather than later.

On Monday, I called Great River Tackle, thanked them for the information they provided the previous week, and gave them my own fishing report. It was the neighborly thing to do and may help another angler catch some fish.

Helping a Fishing Friend

In July, Rodger and I went to Oak Creek near Tinkersville, Pennsylvania to try to catch a few trout. Early July is a little late in the season for trout as the water would be warmer than trout normally like.

We ate breakfast at the Arcadian Restaurant in Tinkersville as usual. The place was packed. We had the window table on the right. I was on a low carbohydrate diet at the time, so I only had one piece of toast with my breakfast. Rodger was recovering from diverticulitis so he ate sparingly, too. This was unlike our previous visits where we chowed down on pancakes and eggs. I brought my digital camera along on this trip and took pictures of the Arcadian, inside and outside, as well as other locations.

Over breakfast, Rodger told me that he had been involuntarily retired for the last six months because he could not find a job. I already knew this because his wife had told my wife when we had dinner together a while ago. This was the first time he actually acknowledged this to me. I think that his pride kept him from confiding in me until now. He told me that he was really stressed over this and believed that this had helped bring on his diverticulitis, along with some strawberries that he had eaten. He also said that he was discriminated against for a job because he was 64 years old. He was near tears when he told me this.

He was a company sales representative all his life, but he was also a civilian pilot. He learned how to fly in the U.S. Navy, and practiced these skills as a search and rescue pilot in Vietnam. I asked him if he could teach class or become a pilot/ground school instructor. He said that had called around various airports and universities and was told that times are bad and they are not looking for class instructors of any kind. He said that he kept pounding on doors but had no luck. I told him that one definition of insanity was to keep doing the same thing and expecting different results! He laughed.

I then asked, "If the only thing open to you is to work for yourself as a manufacturer's representative, what would be the ideal position?" He said that it had to be fun, part time, a technical product, and one that he could believe in. He said he does not have to make a full salary.

I told him that there was a local job seekers organization that meet twice a month, and that they had more than 3,300 on their email list.

"Why don't you go to a meeting, sign up for the internet site access, and send out an email to all 3,300 members, stating your requirements and asking for suggestions," I said. "Why don't you call the local business incubator and ask if any start-up needs a part time sales or marketing person? You should also look at the annual list of 100 fastest growing companies in our area for ideas," I added. He thought that these were great ideas.

I asked Rodger about his ruby ring that he always wears. He told me an uncle, who had been in WWII bought it in France in 1945, had given it to him. This uncle had coached him through this post-traumatic stress after he returned from Vietnam. I told him that to relieve my stress, I fish and coach job seekers.

"Why don't you call the Veterans Administration and offer to coach those solders returning from Iraq and Afghanistan?" I said. "This would be a good way to relieve your stress," I added.

"It is going to be my personal mission to help you find a job," I declared. He was near tears when we finished talking and left the restaurant.

We normally fish in Oak Creek at one particular access point, and drove there, but before we actually started to fish, we decided to look at four other access points to Pine Creek. We knew about them but had never assessed them to determine how good they might be. The creek at the Seldom Seen Road access point was only about five feet across and under very old and large hemlock trees, which cast deep, dark shadows over the entire forest floor including the stream. An angler would need a short rod to fish in there. The other access points looked okay and we selected another and started fishing there.

About 275 feet downstream from where we parked our car, I caught a 14 inch rainbow on a #14 Pine Creek Sparkle nymph attached to my tippet about 8 inches below a 'thingamabobber' strike indicator. This spot is now marked on my GPS map for Tinkersville. This site has large hemlock trees hanging over and covering the water.

The stream was slightly high and muddy. The weather was rain showers on and off all day, with an air temperature 65°F, and the water temperature of 57°F.

Both Rodger and I saw a dragonfly with a bright blue body and very black wings. It was very striking. You normally do not see bright blue colors in nature, other than some flowers. It had actually landed on Rodger's rod for a while. I looked up this color scheme later on the internet and discovered that we had seen an adult male eastern pondhawk.

After a while, we drove to the primary stream access point and fished there for a while. We did not catch anything but left because the rain began to soak through my fishing shirt. I didn't want to drive back in wet clothes.

We ate at another restaurant in Tinkersville for lunch. The menu had prayers and crosses on it. The waitresses were dressed as, and had hairstyles indicating, they were Mennonite. We went there because it was after 2:30PM and the Arcadian was closed.

On the drive home, we talked about going to the Grand Canyon of Pennsylvania on our next trip, and about Rodger finding his next job. As I was dropping him off at his house, I recalled that he had initiated the conversation to go on this fishing trip. Maybe this entire trip was not to catch fish but to ask for help.

Fish Bites

Reader's Note: This is a BONUS story, written for the author's grandchildren, and meant to be read to them. It is a chronical of their first and second fishing trips. It was written at a grade school reading level. This story was deliberately included for those readers who have small children or grandchildren of "story book" age. Please delight in reading this story to them. It just may lead to an intergenerational fishing trip! Beginning readers can also enjoy this story by themselves. All other readers should feel free to skip this story without feeling guilty.

****

Two boys, David and William, lived in a nice house on the Great Plains with their mother and father. Their house sat on the prairie, and this meant that the land was very flat, with endless fields all around the small town where they lived. During the summer, these fields are planted and used to grow tall corn stocks or low soybeans. There are a few trees scattered about, mostly around houses and along the borders of the large fields. There are a few ponds and shallow creeks in the area, but the deep kind of water that fish could actually live in all year round is scarce. For these and many other reasons, these boys had never caught a fish near their house before.

The boys' Grandpa lived very far away. Although he loved the boys very much, he only saw them several times a year. He was determined to be with them and help them catch their first fish. Their Grandpa wanted these boys to get the idea of how to fish, so he brought them toy fishing rods years before they actually ever went fishing. As these boys grew he started bringing them real fishing equipment.

The reason that the boys' Grandpa was so interested in fishing was that the Grandpa's Uncle Paul took Grandpa fishing when he was just six years old, and Grandpa caught his first fish. Since then their Grandpa loved to fish. When the boys' Daddy was a little boy, their Grandpa took him to a small pond near their house in Ohio and Daddy caught his first fish. When the boys' Daddy was a young man, their Daddy and their Grandpa met in the Rocky Mountains, and hiked up to the top of a mountain to catch cutthroat trout in a lake above the tree line, but this is another story for another time. The love of fishing was passed down from generation to generation in their family.

Finally, one summer when the boys were 8 and 5½ years old, Grandpa thought very deeply and made a plan. He called and emailed the local fishing Clubs where the boys lived, but these Clubs were no help. The people who belonged to these Clubs fished for big fish in lakes and rivers far away. They said that the fishing was not very good near where the boys lived. Their Grandpa was very unhappy to learn this. He did not want to drive very far to take the boys fishing. Next, Grandpa called the forest and park rangers in the county, where the boys lived.

"Where can I take my grandsons fishing? We want to catch lots of fish," Grandpa asked them.

"Go to the dock on the lake at River Bow Preserve," said the ranger. Grandpa realized that this lake was just outside a nearby city, and he could drive there in only 15 minutes from the boys' house.

"The park opens at 7:00AM, but do not arrive before that time, because the park ranger on duty will not open the gate to the park until then," added the ranger. "Small bass and bluegill will bite at the dock from 7:00AM to 8:00AM in the morning. These fish will bite on small hooks using small bait."

"Thank you very much," said Grandpa. He was very excited to learn this.

Grandpa then decided to buy the boys new fishing rods and reels to help them catch fish. Grandpa also brought size 10 and 12 hooks with him. These hooks are very small. He thought that they would work well to catch the fish that the park ranger told him about. It is a funny fact that the larger the hook number, the smaller the hook size.

Daddy bought his fishing license at an outdoor store in town. He also bought one-inch long mealworms to use as bait. The store wanted to sell Daddy minnows or night crawlers as bait to catch large fish. But their Daddy said they wanted to catch small fish. This confused the store clerk.

Grandpa also bought his fishing license at this same store. Grandpa's fishing license cost $15.50 for a three-day non-resident license. When Grandpa arrived at the boys' house, he gave them their new fishing rods. William and David liked them very much.

Grandpa, Daddy, David and William made a plan. They decided to go to fishing the next morning. Grandpa then programmed his handheld GPS to find the fishing spot.

All the fishermen got up very early, about 6:00AM, and got dressed to go fishing. Grandpa wore his lucky fishing hat. They put fishing rods and reels in the car, and left the house about 20 minutes before 7:00AM. They drove to the fishing spot in Mommy's car. Daddy drove, but Grandpa used his GPS to guide them right up to the front gate of the park. In addition, there was a sign on the road with an arrow pointing to the park entrance.

On the way to the fishing spot, they all talked about how they were going to "out-trick" the fish.
"I am going to out-trick the fish," said William.
"I am going to out-trick the fish," said David.
"We are all going to out-trick the fish," said Grandpa. "But who is going to catch the most fish?"
"I am!" said William.
"I am!" said David.
"Yes, maybe you will," said Grandpa. "But I have a lucky fishing hat, so maybe I will catch the most fish today."

One of the boys held the mealworm bait box on his lap during the trip to the park, making sure that they were still alive. They joked that they going to tell Mommy that we let some fishing worms loose in her car!

They arrived at the entrance to the park at 7:00AM. The gate was still closed. They had to wait for the park ranger to open the gate. While they waited, they drove over a bridge on the Sangamon River, which was nearby, and Grandpa told a story about how Abraham Lincoln and his cousin John Hanks cleared the land, split tree trunks to make rail fences, and built a farm in 1830, downstream from the part of the river we were looking at. When they got back to the gate, there was a man already there in a pickup truck hitched to a trailer with a boat on it. He was waiting to drive into the park. The park ranger arrived at eight minutes after 7:00AM and opened the gate. They followed the man with the boat along a narrow park road, which ended in a parking lot.

They parked the car and watched this fisherman, and one other, put their boats into the lake. The fishermen backed their boat trailers, with the boats on them, down a ramp right into the lake. The boats were untied from the trailer and let float onto the lake. The boys got their fishing equipment out of the back of the car and walked down to the lake. Grandpa baited the small hooks. He divided the one-inch mealworms into four parts because the hooks were so small.

The boys fished off the end and sides of a floating aluminum pier. They dropped their bobbers in the shadow side of the pier, out of the sunlight, starting just after 7:00AM. Grandpa measured the air temperature. It was 74°F. The sky was part sunny and part cloudy. David helped Grandpa measure the temperature of the water. The water temperature was 78°F. Grandpa wrote down this information in his fishing journal.

A roof covered part of the pier. When people were not there, birds must have sat in the rafters of this roof, because they left bird do-do all over the table underneath this roof. This reminded Grandpa of "The Little Birdies Song." One couple watched the boys fish for a while.

William caught four fish: two bluegill and two bass. William's first fish was six inches long. Grandpa and Daddy took pictures of the fish. The fish William caught flopped on the dock as Grandpa tried to get them off William's hook. Grandpa scooped up the fish with his bare hands to return him safely to the water.

David did not catch anything because all the fish were tugging at, and eating his worm without actually biting on the end of the hook. They were trickier than he was. David tried and tried to catch them. David's bobber kept going under the water but he could not catch these fish.

"These are robber fish," declared David. They were indeed robber fish, because they were stealing the mealworms without being caught!
"We really need smaller size hooks, size 14 or smaller, to catch these robber fish," said Grandpa. David agreed.
"I think that the smaller fish aren't that smart, and we could catch them," David said.

While we were fishing, David noticed Grandpa's lucky fishing hat. David really liked Grandpa's lucky fishing hat, but he did not have a fishing hat of his own.

"Grandpa, would you buy me a lucky fishing hat?" David asked Grandpa. Grandpa promised that he would. Grandpa brought special sunglasses with him fishing to let him see the fishes under the water. David wore these glasses so he could spot the fishes, which he did.

William said, "I am the fishing champion because I caught four fishes." And he was, because neither Grandpa, Daddy nor David caught any fishes. We guessed that we fed the fishes about 15 mealworms. We kept the rest of the worms in case we wanted to go back again.

The boys saw four boats on the lake while they were there. Each boat contained only one fisherman. The sun rose higher in the sky. After a while, the fish did not bite anymore, so they stopped fishing. They put their fishing gear in the car, and drove out of the park at about 9:30 AM.

After fishing, they went directly to the hamburger restaurant in the nearest town to discuss everything they remembered about this fishing adventure. This restaurant was only a few minutes' drive away and next to the highway. They boys washed their hands first and then Daddy ordered chocolate milk and apple chips for both David and William. Daddy had a coke and Grandpa had a muffin breakfast. They talked about what happened on the fishing trip. To help write this story, Grandpa wrote in his fishing journal what everyone remembered.

When the fishermen arrived home, the boys told Mommy and Grandma all about their fishing trip. Mommy took a picture of all the fishermen standing on the front porch. Grandpa counted more than two dozen mealworms left in the bait box. The box was then put in the refrigerator to help keep the mealworms alive.

At lunchtime William, David, Grandma and Grandpa went to McAlister's restaurant for lunch. Near McAlister's restaurant was a large fishing store. After lunch, David, William and Grandpa went into this store and bought size 14 bait hooks to catch the robber fish. These hooks were smaller than what they used that the morning.

"These hooks will give us a good chance to catch the robber fish," said David.

In the afternoon, David whispered in Grandpa's ear, "Can we go fishing again?"

"I would be willing to go, but you have to ask your Daddy," replied Grandpa.

When David asked his Daddy, Daddy said, "Yes!"

David asked William, "Do you want to go fishing again?"

"Yes," said William.

They all agreed to go fishing again that evening. They did not need to buy any more mealworms, because they still had enough left over from the morning.

The hooks they bought did not have a leader on them. Because they planned to use these hooks that evening, they had to tie a leader to the hook eye. A leader is a short length of fishing line that has to be fastened to the hook with a fisherman's knot. The leader has a loop on the other end, which is used to snap onto the fishing line.

Grandpa went down to the basement in David's and William's house to start tying these knots. Grandpa put each hook in a small vice and shined a strong light on the hook to help him see better. William also went to the basement to watch, so Grandpa taught him how to tie these knots. When William learned to tie this knot, he showed his Daddy. After some practice William became very good at tying these knots.

"William, if you can tie these knots, then tying a fly is not much more difficult," said Grandpa.

"Grandpa, will you teach me to tie a fly?" asked William.

"Yes," said Grandpa, "I will teach you how to tie a fly."

"Can we keep my first fly to show and not use it?" asked William.

"Yes," said Grandpa, "I have a shadow box that we can use. Maybe we can also have a sign made to put on the box."

The fishermen left David's and William's house at about 7:30 PM to drive to the same fishing spot. The sun was low in the sky. The park had a sign that said it closes at 9:00PM. They knew that the park ranger would lock the gate until the next morning. They arrived at the park before 8:00PM. This gave them at least one hour to catch some fish.

They parked the car the same place as in the morning, and walked out to the end of the same pier that they fished from that morning. Each boy carried his rod. Grandpa then put the size 14 hook on the end of David's and William's fishing lines, and small pieces of mealworms, too.

"This time we were going to out-trick the tricky robber fish," said David.

The boys started fishing. When it happened, Grandpa was watching David's rod. David was talking to his Daddy about 25 feet away. Grandpa noticed that David's bobber was under the water.

"Oh, David you caught a fish," Grandpa called out. David came running down the dock and pulled his rod and bobber up. There was a fish on the end of his line! David caught the first fish of the evening. He had out-tricked the robber fish! Daddy and Grandpa each took a picture of David with his fish. David was very happy.

When Grandpa tried to take the fish off David's line, the fish started wiggling and jumped onto the dock. It started flopping around. David jumped back.
"That creeps me out," said David.
Grandpa scooped up the fish with his bare hands and tossed him into the lake.

William caught the next fish, bringing his total to five fish for the day. David then caught the next fish bringing his total to two for the day. David caught the most fish in the evening and was declared the champion of the second fishing trip. One of the robber fish was a bluegill and the other one was a small bass. But William caught the most fish for the whole day.

The sun was going down and the shadows on the water were getting longer. It was near the time that the boys had to leave the park. Just before they left for home, Grandpa took out his fly rod and put it together. With this rod, he cast a popper fly a very long way, about 75 feet, from the pier into the weeds near the shore. David and William could not believe how far Grandpa could cast a fly.

"Will you show me how to do that?" William asked Grandpa.
"Yes," said Grandpa, with a smile.
"Grandpa, I hope you catch a fish on your fly line," said David.
"I hope so too!" said Grandpa.

Grandpa was hoping to catch a large bass. He knew that these large fish liked to feed on smaller fish that swim in the weeds near shore just before dark. Grandpa cast his fly about two dozen times, but no bass came to bite on Grandpa's fly. Grandpa did not catch any fish this day, even though he was wearing his lucky fishing hat.

Before William and David left the dock, they dumped the remaining mealworms into the lake for the fish to eat. They walked off the dock and up the path to their car in the parking lot. As they were leaving, they saw a woman catch a fish from the same boat launch dock where they saw some men put their boats into the lake that morning. They drove out of the park at 8:45 PM.

On the way home, everyone was very happy. The tiny hooks worked well to catch the robber fish. William, David and Grandpa told jokes to Daddy. They told him that the dock was made out of "Muni Mula". This is actually "aluminum" spelled backwards. Daddy did not know this. We also told him this joke:

Grandpa: "William, did you change the fish's water today?"
William: "No, I didn't."
Grandpa: "Why not?"
William: "Because they did not use up all the water I gave them yesterday!"

On the way home, some fireworks filled the sky. They also saw many birds. By the time they arrived home, it was completely dark.

On this day, David and William became real fishermen. The next day, Grandpa left a message on the kitchen table for William to read. It said:

"The fisherman may forget most of the fish that he catches,
But he never forgets the people he caught them with,
Or the streams and lakes in which they were caught."

Before Grandpa and Grandma drove home, lucky fishing hats were discussed. Both William and David said they wanted *Indiana Jones*-style hats.

"Could I have a red feather for my lucky fishing hat?" asked David.

"Yes," said Grandpa.

"I would like a patch of white fur for my hat to put my flies on," William said.

"Okay," said Grandpa.

That Pigeon Is Fast

I was a life-long graphite rod fly fisherman and had never owned or even touched a bamboo rod before 2002. Then, I accidentally came across an old bamboo fly rod. One of the tips was split and the rod was in relatively bad shape. The rod sock was dry rot. Guides were missing or tarnished. I was curious as to how a bamboo rod felt to cast, so I bought it anyway and took it to a famous local cane rod maker. We struck a deal for him to restore it. He reported that it was made circa 1933 and has collectable value. Instead of keeping it safe and on display, I use it on the stream, because of how it feels in my hand. I then began consciously looking for old bamboo fly rods in poor condition.

Two years later, I came across a second rod, and purchased it. When I took it to the same rod maker, he refused to restore it, saying that it had no collectable value, and that it was not worth his time. I was disappointed because I had planned to give it to my college-age daughter, who had been my fly fishing companion on many trips. Then I had a sudden burst of inspiration.

"I will buy all the parts from you if you teach me how to restore the rod," I said.

"Okay," the rodmaker agreed. "Buy three books on making fly rods: Handcrafting Bamboo Fly Rods by Wayne Cattanach, A Master's Guide to Building a Bamboo Fly Rod by Hoagy Carmichael, and Fundamentals of Building a Bamboo Fly-Rod by George Mauer. Read them and call me back," he added. I agreed to do this.

Although the books were daunting at first and it took me three months, I did read them. Fortunately, I have a degree in engineering and could understand many of the manufacturing techniques, and the technical reasons for them.

I made an appointment to meet him, purchased all the parts, and asked him many questions about what I had read, which he was gracious enough to answer. In the last decade I have taken that knowledge and restored and repaired more than a few bamboo fly rods for friends. My rod making skills improved dramatically as I undertook this work.

In 2014, I purchased a Payne #100 taper bamboo rod blank to build into a customized rod to present to my grandson as a Christmas present. The day after Christmas I took him outside and taught him to cast to a four count rhythm (like in A River Runs Through It). He is only six years old, but out of his first three dozen casts, one was bad, ten were perfect and the balance were good casts. He almost couldn't make a bad cast with this rod. I had not expected this and was astonished to say the least. The slow action of this rod forgives most casting mistakes.

The Payne #100 taper was developed by Jim Payne and first sold by the E.F. Payne Company in 1931. It is considered one of the 10 best tapers of all time. When I first cast this rod, I fell in love with it.

I am a serial entrepreneur and own several successful corporations, but am approaching retirement age and decided that I would seize this opportunity to turn my passion for fly fishing into yet another business. So I started a split cane bamboo fly rod manufacturing company to be my retirement company. I designed and had made five fixtures and machines to automate my hand labor, and started making rods. I hired a part-time apprentice to help with the wood shaping, and a retired woman with sewing skills, to do rod wrapping.

This company specializes in hand crafting split cane bamboo fly rods using vintage tapers. I decided to copy famous old rod designs rather than develop my own taper. These rods are precision reproductions of the finest and most famous bamboo rods ever made. They are intended for regular use on the water, and I anticipate that they will also become a treasured family heirloom for generations of fishermen.

Bamboo rods perform unlike any other rod available. They load, cast, and respond with a sweetness and finesse that cannot be achieved with graphite or fiberglass. These rods offer perhaps the finest experience a fly fisher can have by replicating what are considered to be the top ten tapers ever conceived and crafted in the history of bamboo rod making.

The company offers 10 different rods, each with its own unique characteristics such as the Leonard 38, Payne 100, Phillipson Pacemaker, Winston, Garrison 206, Hardy CCdeFrance, Paul Young Perfectionist, Thomas and Thomas Caneus, Dickerson 7012, Granger Aristocrat, and Orvis Wes Jordan.

Originals of these rods in good condition currently sell for $3,500 to beyond $5,000 on the internet. Production of these rods enable my customers to fish with their own bamboo rod for the price of mid-level graphite rod.

I believe that there is no greater graceful and beautiful rod than one crafted from split bamboo. They look good and they feel good. I try to make each model as faithful to the original as I can and to each other, comparing and getting the dimensions to within one thousandth of an inch along the entire taper. Even with this attention to detail, each rod of the same model is unique, like a fingerprint. Each one has its own unique characteristic. Other rods, graphite, boron, glass, and steel, mass produced on machines are truly identical. I can only attribute the differences between bamboo rods to slight variations in the bamboo fibers from the different culms.

I have a good memory, but it is not that good to remember the precise "feel" of a rod. In comparing tapers, I kind of cheat. For example, I keep a copy of each of my 4-weight rods. When I make a new 4-weight for the first time, I bring all of them along to my secret scientific test area (read parking lot in front of the building in which I am a tenant). Sometimes I have to dodge cars going by. My neighbors think I am crazy. My company actually makes electronic micro-sensors. And that I what I do in my day job.

I then compare casting the tapers to each other. I keep switching rods to my casting hand in seconds. I then mentally place the rods in order from slowest to fastest. Of course, this does not take into account many other factors, and subtleties. Once I have done this, I only have to remember how the new taper fits into this order. It is still fun for me to do this.

I was raised on graphite, but the feel of even the Payne #100 (very slow) is poetry. A well-known bamboo fly rod maker and certified casting instructor cast my Payne #100 copy 110 feet at a trade show we both attended last year. I was mesmerized by his perfect rhythm and the whisper and whooshing sounds of his casting technique. He put the rod back into my hand and asked me to cast it. I could not cast my own rod that far, maybe a wildly inaccurate 75 feet at the most.

"You can't cast," were the first words out of his mouth. "How much do you practice?" he added.

"I never practice," I answered. "I only cast when I am on a stream."

"That's your problem," he said. "Practice 10 minutes a day and you'll do fine." I just laughed knowing how impossible this would be for me.

Now I keep a rod with reel and line in a stand near the front door of my company offices. Whenever I feel the urge, I go out and cast it for a few minutes. It's not every day, and not 10 minutes, but more often than never. I can hit a manhole cover almost every time at 60 feet. I mostly fish at distances closer than this anyway. My goal is a decent presentation, and I am not out to win a tournament distance casting championship.

In addition to making new rods, I also restore and repair bamboo rods, which brings me to the pigeon. I had just restored an old bamboo rod for a customer, and was presenting it to him over lunch at a restaurant in the next town south of mine. He loved it.

"What's your story," I asked, after lunch and some pleasantries.

"I worked for more than twenty years as the Environmental Compliance Manager for a steel corporation," he said. "But I am retired now. I actually have a PhD in biology, and that education served me well in my profession."

"What do you do now for excitement?" I asked.

"Well, I love to fly fish, of course, but my biggest passion is racing homing pigeons. I win almost every race I enter." I knew that people raced homing pigeons, but had never met anyone who had actually done this.

"That's a pretty tall claim," I responded. "How do you do that?"

"Well, I game the system," he said.

"What!" I laughed. "I didn't know that you could dope pigeons."

"Nothing like that," he answered. "I do two things that invariably work. You have to know that pigeons are gregarious, they flock together. It's instinct. Millions of years of evolution, for mutual protection against predators."

"This means that most pigeons will fly together as a flock for as long as they can, before feeling the urge to veer off to come home. Since they are not flying directly home, this adds to their race time. To counteract this I raise my pigeons to be anti-social."

"How do you raise a pigeon to be anti-social?" I asked in astonishment.

"That's another discussion for another time," he answered. "The second thing I do is race female pigeons who are sitting on a nest of eggs."

"The maternal instinct," I said, as a reasonable guess.

"Yes, but with a big boost," he added. "I take one of her eggs the night before the race, make a hole in one end, and empty the yolk out of the egg. I then catch a bottlenose fly, and put it in the egg through the hole. I tape up the hole, and put the egg back in her nest."

"All night long the egg is moving and vibrating. The female pigeon thinks that this egg is just about to hatch."

"When I take her the next morning to the start of the race, she is frantic to get back to her nest to nurture the chick she is expecting to come out of the hatching egg," he explained.

"Works almost every time," he concluded.

"Wow!" I said in complete amazement. I did believe that he could win a lot of homing pigeon races with these tactics. Then I struck me. "What am I going to do with this information? It's taking up space in my brain and I will never be able to forget it either."

Somehow "gaming the system" did not seem to be one of Aesop's fables that I remembered from my childhood, and the only positive moral I could draw from this story was, " In all things, seek the initiative."

Suddenly I laughed, when I realized that this is one of the main reasons that I build rods, to meet people and hear their stories. Sure, the company makes a little money, but the pleasure comes from creating something useful and beautiful, and the endlessly fascinating interactions with people. To see their response to a rod unwrapped and revealed for the first time. And to hear their stories.

Why I Fly Fish

This is a complex intellectual, emotional and even philosophical question. I fly fish because it is simultaneously an intellectual and physical challenge. It fully engages both mind and body. It is exciting. It is relaxing.

It requires my creativity and forces me to constantly learn new things to improve (observation of environmental conditions, life cycles of fish and insects, fly patterns, how to read the water, and casting and presentation techniques). It lets me connect with and enjoy the beauty of nature. It is an excuse to go out into the woods or mountains, or onto creeks, streams, rivers and lakes.

I fly fish to enjoy the camaraderie of good friends, and meet people with similar interests and passions. It is an instant bond with people I have never met before. It connects me with the generations before me and after me. It provides me with anticipation, fun, mystery and adventure in my life.

I fly fish because it fulfils something deep in me I cannot obtain from any other activity, and these experiences have made my life richer and fuller.

Fishing Tips and Tales

About the Author

William King never won any literary awards, although the other students in his fifth grade class loved his comic strips in their student newspaper. He graduated from Lehigh University with a degree in Electrical Engineering and earned a Master's Degree in Business Administration from the University of Pittsburgh. None of this has anything to do with these stories. He started keeping a fishing journal in 1996 to preserve some technical information about fishing trips and tackle. But at some point, it changed to include preserving memories of a lifetime of fishing. When he began writing, he had no idea that real life could turn into literature.

The information he was initially preserving was how to tie various flies, dates of fishing trips, locations, weather and stream conditions, what was caught, and with what flies. He also recorded who went with him and any other brief thoughts. After a while, he realized that reading these notes about old trips let him relive some good times. So with no literary background, experience, or even any specific encouragement, he vowed to continue this activity and actually write more stories. He has continued this practice for many years, and up to now, has only shared them with his family, friends, and a few other people that he could forcefully persuade to read them. However, he has been known to tell fishing stories of doubtful veracity to anyone within earshot.

The fishing stories within these covers are meant for the readers' enjoyment, but he also wanted to leave a legacy to his children and grandchildren. He lives in a small town in Ohio with his wife of more than 40 years who puts up with all his fishing, rod building, fly tying, storytelling, and writing activities with love and good humor.